Burying the Typewriter

From pages in the files headed PHOTOGRAPHIC EVIDENCE

"After we lifted the plastic sack we saw in the hole a plastic white container, buried 40 cm deep."

Stamp of the Socialist Republic of Romănia and the signature of Colonel Coman, in charge of penal research

"Represents a typewriter, after it was taken out of its container. The typewriter is an 'Erika' model 115, series 6368642, made in the Democratic Republic of Germany (East Germany)."

The stamp of the Socialist Republic of Romănia and the signature of Colonel Coman; the stamp of CNSAS

Bugan, Carmen.
Burying the typewriter
: a memoir /
c2012.
3330522933 7
gi   1/14/12

Burying the Typewriter

A MEMOIR

*

Carmen Bugan

Graywolf Press

Copyright © 2012 by Carmen Bugan

This publication is made possible in part by a grant provided by the Minnesota State Arts Board, through an appropriation by the Minnesota State Legislature from the Minnesota general fund and the arts and cultural heritage fund with money from the vote of the people of Minnesota on November 4, 2008, and a grant from the Wells Fargo Foundation Minnesota. Significant support has also been provided by the National Endowment for the Arts; Target; the McKnight Foundation; and other generous contributions from foundations, corporations, and individuals. To these organizations and individuals we offer our heartfelt thanks.

Published by Graywolf Press
250 Third Avenue North, Suite 600
Minneapolis, Minnesota 55401

All rights reserved.

www.graywolfpress.org

Published in the United States of America

ISBN 978-1-55597-617-0

2 4 6 8 9 7 5 3 1
First Graywolf Printing, 2012

Library of Congress Control Number: 2012936218

Cover design: Kimberly Glyder Design

For my son, Stefano, and for my daughter, Alisa

We stood among
Those who owned their land, spoke
Of our homelands as if they were reachable

From "At a Gathering of Refugees"

Visiting the Country of My Birth

The tyrant and his wife were exhumed
For proper burial; it is twenty years since
They were shot against a wall in Christmas snow.

*

The fish in the Black Sea are dead. Waves roll them
To the beach. Tractors comb the sand. We stand at water's edge
Whispering, glassy-eyed, throats parched from heat.

Stray dogs howl through nights like choirs
Of mutilated angels, circle around us on hill paths,
Outside gas stations, shops, streets, in parking lots.

Farther, into wilderness, we slow down where horse
And foal walk home to the clay hut by themselves,
Cows cross roads in evenings alone, bells clinking.

People sit on wooden benches in front of their houses,
Counting hours until darkness, while
Shadows of mountains caress their heads.

On through hot dust of open plane, to my village:
A toothless man from twenty years ago
Asks for money, says he used to work for us.

*

I am searching for prints of mare's hooves in our yard
Between stable and kitchen window, now gone
With the time my two feet used to fit inside one hoof.

We sit down to eat on the porch when two sparrows
Come flying in circles over the table, low and fast, happily!
"My grandparents' souls" I think aloud, but my cousin says:

"No, the sparrows have nested under eaves, look
Past the grapevine." Nests big as cupped hands, twigs
And straw. Bird song skids in the air above us.

Into still-remaining rooms no sewing machine,
Or old furniture with sculpted flowers on walnut wood.
No rose bushes climbing window sills, outside.

And here, our water well, a vase of cracked cement. Past
Ghosts of lilac, pear, and quince in the sun-bitten yard I step
On re-imagined hooves, pull the chain, smell wet rust.

Unblemished sky ripples inside the tin bucket,
Cradled in my arms the way I used to hold
Warm goose eggs close to skin so not to break them:

"The earth will remember you" my grandparents once said.
Here, where such dreams do not come true, I have come
To find hoof-prints as well as signs from sparrows.

România, July 2010

Contents

Foreword

It is fairly common these days to find a preponderance of agony memoirs in a pile of nonfiction manuscripts. Suffering seems to sell, so why not have a go at it? one might ask. Well, it can be tiresome, for one thing. For another, suffering in itself is not interesting. If such a memoir is to float, the suffering must be part of something larger and more significant than itself. It must be wound into a larger context, a life in a world, a world with a history. And, more than this, that world should be exposed without self-pity, and without a hint of self-righteousness either.

Such a world is the one described in Carmen Bugan's *Burying the Typewriter*—România in the clutches of its Communist rulers. Here is a world in which Bugan's father, a celebrated anti-Ceaușescu activist, is not to be veered off the path of righteousness. Even when he is safely out of România and in exile in Michigan, his prize photograph in the family album remains the one focused on himself. It is the one in which, as his daughter describes it, he "reenacted his protest against Ceaușescu . . . [leaving] us to God's will and the secret police."

It is the children of political dissidents who can have the hardest time of it. Not only must they compete for their parents' attention with a cause higher than themselves, but they may also find themselves seriously endangered by the cause their parents champion, suffering, at the very least, the disapproval, suspicion, and hostility of their acquaintances, and, at the worst, starvation, abandonment, and death.

And yet the children themselves can be torn. In Bugan's case, there is both resentment and love for a father who, one moment, might romp joyously with his children in the sea, or row them out to Ovid's island, scene of the poet's exile; in the next, endanger them by typing antigovernment pamphlets on an illegal typewriter; and, in yet another, stagger forward in prisoner's chains, tearful at the sight of his starving daughter.

Because the family is endangering the whole village, its members are treated like pariahs by all but the decent few. One of the latter is the literature teacher, who imperils herself by taking the starving Carmen into her office each day to give her a sandwich she has hidden in her handbag. "I can show no gratitude except by eating her food. With time, she will become the reason I believe that literature truly nourishes the hungry. She will become the reason I love morphology and syntax. . . . I will never, for the rest of my life, know or love a teacher more."

By contrast, the history teacher orders Carmen to stand up in class, "declaring, 'Your father is a mentally ill criminal who is destroying your future.'" On the playground, the other children, encouraged by the teacher, taunt her and throw stones at her, calling her "daughter of criminal."

Then there is the blame, the rage leveled at the father by the family itself. At the age of seventeen, Carmen tells him, "'I never wanted to be part of your vision. . . . You just took our support without even as much as a word of thanks.'" And she is not alone. Her mother, someone whose "ambitions have never leapt higher than to walk the length of our village and be greeted warmly by everyone," also finds it hard to forgive him.

And yet, looking back on that time in *Burying the Typewriter*, Carmen Bugan delivers neither a memoir of blame nor a hagiography. What she has drawn, within the story of her own childhood, is a complex portrait of an exasperating father, a man who happens to be a hero in the eyes of Amnesty International and the Western world, a hero in the service of a just cause. But while he may be the driving force behind her story, he is not the subject of it; she is. It is her world that is revealed here, a world that she was forced to leave behind and that she looks back on now with sorrow, pride, longing, and rage.

Exile is an old story. And yet, properly told, it always seems new. *Burying the Typewriter* seems new in this way. It is the passionate story of a village girl caught up in political events beyond her control or understanding. "Well, goodbye, my village," Carmen says as she is leaving. "'*Mînă caii,* Neculai,' I say to myself again, pretty certain that none of the roads will be dusty or small or recognizable from here on."

Lynn Freed
Bakeless Prize Judge

Acknowledgments

Names and events mentioned in this book are true and presented in accordance with my memory. Somewhere I heard someone say that one can trust a book of fiction better than a memoir. I can see how this can be true, especially of a memoir, as opposed to an autobiography. Any fault in recollection in the present book is therefore, happily, mine.

I have no intention to pass judgment, to bring shame to anyone, or to engage in discrediting the character of the particular secret police (Securitate) staff assigned to my family. The Securitate operated during the Cold War period in România in order to protect the interests of the Communist government, and of President Nicolae Ceaușescu, at the height of the oppression in the 1980s. I hope that the archival material at the end of this book will provide a good hint of the political context of my memories if not also an illustration that politics and the personal cannot be separated at all in some periods of history.

Permission to publish the archival material was given by my family. Thanks are also due to the National Council for the Study of the Archives of the Securitate (CNSAS) in București, which gave me access to my father's files. The CNSAS has reassured me that I can publish the entirety of the files and also the photos and that I can use the real names of people in the files. The document they cited in their conversation with me is OUG24/2008 approved by the Law 293/2008 available in *Monitorul Oficial.* As CNSAS has refused to give me an official permission letter, saying it is not necessary, I take their verbal statement in good faith. Except for the ranked officers of the Securitate and the police, almost everyone, including my father, has a code name—his is "Andronic"—and only now I am beginning to receive letters about the real identity of the informers.

A slightly different version of one of the chapters was a finalist in the New Writing Ventures Awards 2007 (UK) and has been published on the contest's website, and an earlier version of another chapter has been published in the *International Literary Quarterly* online. The poem "Visiting the Country of My Birth" won a commendation in the National Poetry Competition 2010 (UK) and has been published on the Poetry Society's website. I wish to express my profound gratitude to Wolfson College, Oxford University, for awarding me a creative arts fellowship in literature during which I wrote this memoir.

Burying the Typewriter

Old Photographs

Every few weeks my mother rearranges the family pictures around the house. She also moves the beds and the rugs, and she places every movable desk in front of a different window. Then she calls me. My father builds a new garage in every house we buy, but it's never about the garage. He takes his favorite photos of us to the shops, enlarges and frames them, setting them between the tools and around the car crane. Lately he turned a summer shed into a writer's hut where he spends his time drafting letters to the presidents of the world. He tells them about the rotten state of forgetting to which he has been condemned since we emigrated to America.

Since we moved into Thelma's basement on November 17, 1989, the snowy evening when we first landed in America, I must have moved again at least fifteen times. Whenever I go home I argue with my parents about not wanting to build a house in their backyard with my brother and my sister and our husbands. And I clean my parents' house, changing all the pictures around the walls. Then I call my mother at work to hurry up and come see the new arrangement. My brother chose a career in the U.S. Army, my sister still wants to be a traveling nurse, and I have lived in America, Ireland, and England, and on the French-Swiss border, writing poems about wanting to be rooted to one place that I will never leave.

My father's prize photograph is the one in which he reenacted his protest against Ceaușescu and the Communist regime in România in 1983, when he left us to God's will and the secret police, the Securitate.

He posed for us on Helen Street with an American car, on which he placed our Dacia's license plate number (2GL 666). On top of the car, at the front, there is a black placard on which he painted, in big white capital letters, *CĂLĂULE, NU TE VREM CONDUCĂTOR: Criminal, We Don't Want You to Lead Us.* At the back of the car there is a similar placard reading, in translation, *Army, Justice, Police, What Do You Defend, the Ceaușescu Dynasty or the Rights and the Liberty of Man?* He is wearing the same black suit he had on when he demonstrated in 1983, was released from prison in the general amnesty of 1988, and wore on the train between Tecuci and Rome at the end of 1989 when we were expelled from the country with death threats, as we began our exile to Michigan. On his chest he has pinned a piece of paper on which is typed *I Fight for Human Rights.* And he is holding on to a gargantuan portrait of Ceaușescu that he has decorated with black ribbons and the Romanian flag, to symbolize the death of the tyrant's reign. Every time I introduce my father to my friends he wants to talk about this, and when he knows there is a chance of meeting someone new he takes a small print of this picture with him as his passport to show that he is not just any old immigrant.

In my mother's bedroom there is now a black-and-white photo of my sister and me dressed up for a children's show in kindergarten: the show at the village hall, where I recited my first poem on stage and sang a song about mushrooms dancing with their red-and-white polka-dot hats in the forest. On top of my head I have a big, peony-like white bow, which I try to balance while smiling widely at the camera. My sister has a hat that looks like a mushroom cap. This photograph, as all the others, is *forced* on the walls on West River Drive: it is the kind of old that makes you think your life (the version in which you are in the present together with the version from the old pictures) is invented. I remember being young and putting our photographs on the walls of the house we built with my parents, room by room, picture by picture, golden frames matching brass curtain rods. My sister and I were allowed to choose them and chose places for them, just where we wanted, so our kindergarten picture hung above the bookcase in the hallway, where everyone could see it when they looked at the books.

Our portraits were first taken off the walls when the secret police came to search the house just after my father's protest. I was home with my grandmother, who was summoned by my father before he left, to "spend a little bit of time" with me while Mother was in the hospital after giving complicated birth to my brother; my father said he had to "take a trip for a couple of days." My sister was away at the gymnastics school. When the Securitate plucked the family portraits from the walls and threw them over the blankets and pillows they had pulled from the dressers and the beds, I was twelve years old.

Sometimes when I go home now to Michigan to visit my parents, I take out the Romanian photo albums from the bottom of the stack that Mom keeps in the living room cupboards. My parents have their red album; my sister and I have one green album each. Though everything is in black and white, I remember the colors of the clothes and the dusty green or the sandy green of vacations. I also see now how different from each other's our lives have been. The pictures and the icons, though moving from the walls to a pile of things and then on to various other walls, have turned into stores of riches that nourish us when we feel out of place. They are passageways back in time. I call them "our first inheritance."

Our "second inheritance" is eighteen volumes amounting to nearly one thousand five hundred pages, which I have seen recently at the National Council for the Study of the Archives of the Securitate (CNSAS) in Bucureşti; I was granted access to these files *after* I finished the present book. These are some of the secret files from the penal and informative dossiers kept by the Communist government on my father from 1961 until we emigrated to the United States at the end of 1989, just a few weeks before the revolution. They document his lifetime of political dissidence and his three incarcerations, one of which I witnessed. I do not appear in my father's dossiers, or in the photo showing the buried typewriter on which my parents typed anti-Communist propaganda, or in the log of interrogations. But my heart beats between the lines of the reports; I am just at the edge, a ghost. The story I am telling here is the one with me in it, the story of the last penal dossier. It doesn't include anything of what I have done in the twenty years since we left România, from October 1989 until July 2010, when I was given access to the secret files and I sat with my mother in the archives looking at our lives as if other people had lived them. In this book I want only to talk about my childhood, a childhood in which a typewriter was buried, unearthed, buried, and unearthed again by two people who had children for whom they wanted a better future. So this story starts in the 1970s, a few years after I was born, about the time when I began to have memories and my father's code name was already long established as "Andronic," a name we learned about only last summer.

Bunicu and Bunica: Drăgăneşti, 1975

"*Mină caii,* Neculai! *Mină caii,* Neculai!* Ehhh, heeeh!" I am nearly five years old and Grandpa Neculai with his horse and cart is visiting us at our new house. "Ho, ho, Steluța," I hear him call to the horse, "*prrr,* Steluța," just outside the gate. I bolt out the door straight into his arms.

Dad comes after me, laughing, "Carmenuțo, you sure got good ears!" and he shakes Grandpa's hand.

Grandpa is always wearing the same black dusty suit, only today, because it's not Sunday, he hasn't smoothed his hair with walnut oil, so there is a white mess sticking out of his hat.

"Mom, Mom, Bunicu's here," I shout with my arms coiled around Grandpa's neck, my skin all tickly from his hair.

Mom takes him around the house we bought from the old village priest who moved away. We all go in through the front door, by the jasmine bush. The sitting room still smells like the priest and his wife, incense and old people, but the rest of the house reeks of moth-killing *naftalină* from unpacking.

"The new priest is good," says Grandpa. "He lives near the kindergarten, so he'll get to know the folk, and I hear he spends the day on the porch playing cards with his wife."

Mom sighs, "Oh, the scandal about the old priest!"

*Drive the horses, Neculai!

But I don't listen to the conversation. I wriggle my nose and kiss Grandpa's stubbly cheek: "Can I go home with you?"

"But aren't you going to show Bunicu the house?" asks Mom.

"Sure."

Each room has two doors leading into other rooms. It's a labyrinth of cramped spaces with brooms and shoes in corners and toys strewn in the middle of the bedroom my sister, Loredana, and I share. The kitchen has a very short blue door, so Grandpa has to lower himself as he walks through it; from his arms I grab the top of the lintel. When we're inside, I show him the square hole in a side wall through which the kitchen communicates with the dining room: "This is the spy-window."

Except for the spy-window, my sister and I don't really like the priest's house as much as we like Grandpa and Grandma's house. Loredana, whom I almost always call Dana and Dad calls Dănuța, is one year younger than me but is the tomboy of the family. At Grandpa's house she loves to make the turkey angry until it puffs up its feathers like a barrel and the pale skin-beads around its neck turn all red. She puffs her little body up too and blows her lips at it, screaming, imitating its *clookedoodle* sound and shaking her dark hair. Her eyebrows arch above her black eyes and her red cheeks. Here there isn't much to play with.

Grandpa left his cart outside the gates. When we're all out and I am on the horse, I take Grandpa's black dusty hat, which falls too deeply over my face, wrapping me in the scent of hay and his old sweaty hair. I push the hat to the back of my head so I can see. His blue-gray eyes fill with light, his sculpted cheeks with sun. Everyone roars with laughter when I imitate Grandma Anghelina on trips to the farmers' market in Tecuci: "*Mînă caii,* Neculai!" The horse starts to move obediently. I am thrilled. I want to go home with Grandpa in his cart. Dad takes me from the horse, puts me down. Bunicu kisses my cheek, climbs in without me, and picks up his whip. When he *click-clacks* his tongue, Steluța starts again and I run screaming and crying in the dust raised by the wheels. I try very hard to catch up with them, but I fall behind. Dust comes into my nose and eyes, making me cough and cry more, my sounds rising over the *gluop gluop* of Steluța's hooves.

*

I don't like being with my parents, because they are too strict. I love running my hands over the polished furniture to make fingerprints on the shine of the tables and glass displays, something for which I get punished. Mom is obsessive about cleaning and keeps the shoes-off rule when we're inside. My sister and I are not allowed to bring the cats or the dogs into the house. We must eat at exact times and have big plates of tomato salad after our afternoon naps instead of going straight into the street to play. And we can only play in the street for an hour or two. Plus, Mom always likes to "make observations" about how Loredana and I behave, so we are scolded all the time, something we are not used to. Our grandparents didn't scold us even on the day when the Gypsies came with their cart and asked my sister and me to give them corn in exchange for wild apples. Loredana, my cousin Florin, and I ran to the granary and brought as much corn as we could carry in our shirts. We made many trips back and forth, but when Bunica heard all our clambering around the yard and saw what we were doing, she just told the Gypsies that's enough corn. There are too many rules at my parents' house, so my sister and I want to go to Mom's adoptive parents, my grandparents.

Mom was adopted when she was three, at her mother's funeral. Grandma Anghelina gave her a tablespoon of honey, after which she followed her and Grandpa Neculai all the way to their house. Mom's natural mother died when she gave birth to Mom's youngest sister, who also died. At the funeral, Mom's older sister Balașa, who was already eleven years old, was taken in by an aunt who said she could help with the housework. Mom's natural father had tuberculosis and spent the whole time at the funeral coughing; people knew he couldn't take care of kids. When a couple of years later he was brought to my adoptive grandparents to die, he was kept at the back of the house in the shed and Mom was told to call him "mister" for fear that she would remember him as a father and suffer losing him. Mom's brother Ştefan went to another aunt because he was also older and was useful around the farm. No one wanted my mom because she was too young, so when Grandmother Anghelina saw her running barefoot in the dust after the funeral procession, she felt sorry for her. She sent Grandpa Neculai home to get a jar of honey, and after they gave Mom a table-spoon she didn't want to leave them. I have always known this story.

Bunicu and *bunica,* that's how we say grandfather and grand-mother. Loredana is Bunicu's girl and I am Bunica's, which means that Loredana gets to feed the horse before me and I get to feed the pigeons and the chickens before her. In the mornings, just before the sunrise, when the rooster calls *coo-coo-reee-goo,* Bunica goes straight to the pantry where she keeps sacks of grain and corn. She fills two pots and goes outside barefoot. Sometimes I watch her from the bed, wrapped in the colorful quilts she makes from our old clothes and old sheets. Loredana usually turns to the other side, snoring. Most morn-ings I rush after Bunica on the cold damp earth: we throw handfuls of grain, which sound like rain hitting the bald middle of the yard. Pigeons fly from their nests (which Bunicu looks after and repairs every year), making a cloud of wings over us. And then all the chick-ens, roosters, turkeys, and geese come for the corn. We grab the hens and feel underneath their throats to make sure they are full before we stop feeding. There is so much noise in the yard from hissing geese, little chicks with their tiny beaks and yellow coats, turkeys puffing up and spitting air!

Next we must milk the cow, so Bunica takes her wooden stool and her blue tin pail to the backyard. She talks to the cow softly while she squeezes its teats between her thumb and her forefinger; milk glides warm and fragrant from the depth of her palm, her dress spreading out an imaginary field of blue flowers on her lap. Then we feed the pigs, who smell so awful and look so badly caked in their own shit that I always have to have my sweater lifted to my nose like a mask. My favorite ritual is to collect the eggs from the hens; they are brown and warm and I have to reach into the hay under the hens' butts, which makes them chuckle pleasantly. They are used to my disturbing them in the mornings and evenings. When it's time for making chicks, in the spring, Bunica brings all the eggs in the willow basket to the kitchen table and we look inside them with a lamp, letting the light filter through the yolk to see if there are babies in there. Those eggs we take back to the nests so the hens can sit on them until baby chicks peck their way out. I am fascinated by this. When Bunica says it's happening, I go and watch forever until the shell begins to crack and pieces of it fall on the grass, revealing a tiny beak, and then the chick, astonished with life. They are fuzzy and furry, the little chicks, all bright yellow. They fit in my cupped hands.

So, as I walk back to my parents with my face dirty from dust and tears, I know exactly what I would have done today if Bunicu had taken me home with him. To begin with, it is summer so we would water the big animals at the well, one by one: the cow, the calf, the horse. I love the smell of wet rust coming from the chain and how Bunicu lets me clamber to the edge of the well to look into the water, make faces in it before the bucket drops and the mirrorlike surface breaks into tiny waves. Then I put my hand in the bucket to feel the horse's nose as he snorts while he drinks. After this we fill the wooden boat-like trough for the pigs, then the various rusted pots spread around the yard and under the trees for the hens. When we're done with all this I am soaked. My feet are black from the wet dust I run through. I stomp my feet and tell my mom and dad that they have no horses, no well, no hens, no eggs for me to collect, no pigeons to fly for grain in the mornings and therefore I want to go to Bunicu and Bunica. Mom pretends to cry because I want to leave her but I don't care.

*

Soon we find out we don't have to worry about being away from Bunicu and Bunica for long. We are going to build our own brand-new house in the backyard of the priest's and then demolish the old one. Plus, Mom and Dad, who run the grocery store in Ivești, which is a long drive from Drăgănești, have to be there from morning until late at night. Ivești is a small merchant village with cement houses lined up against the main street and Gypsy shacks in the deep, unpaved back streets. The center is always buzzing with people who mostly shop for food, so my parents see a lot of them at the grocery store, forever asking for Sibiu salami and hard cheese, which are delicacies. The clothing store doesn't have many things to choose from and there everyone hangs around mostly for the gossip, since we all go to seamstresses. My dad also repairs people's radios and TVs to make extra money. His little shop, in a two-room rented house next to the grocery store, belongs to the government, like all the shops and stores, but many ask him privately to go to their homes to fix their radios and TVs. They pay him in kind: with hens, eggs, flour, wine. Ever since I can remember, Mom and Dad are mostly at Ivești. The grocery store takes most of their energy because they have to struggle to get supplies. The food situation is not too bad yet, but, as Dad often says, more food is going to Russia than coming into our kitchens.

My sister and I are used to moving even though we are so young. We were both born in Vrancea, about forty kilometers south of Drăgănești. I have no memories of it; I only know that my parents began their married life there as a modern couple, after Mom gave up her teaching job. Vrancea was Mom's only move away from my grandparents, but my father lived all over the country before my parents were married. He tells all kinds of stories about driving movie reels up mountain roads and showing films in small villages. I must have been about two or three when my parents returned to Bunicu and Bunica and began working at the grocery store in Ivești.

There is an agreement that from the end of the summer my sister and I will go to stay with our grandparents during the week. Mom and Dad will come at the weekends to visit or take us away for a day or two. Bunica Floarea, Dad's mom, will come from Satul Nou to stay at the priest's house, which is just a walk from Bunicu and Bunica's home, in Drăgănești. Bunica Floarea will oversee the deliveries of materials for the building work. We will have lots of places to explore and a whole new grandmother to play with when we come back to our new house!

*

Kindergarten is five doors down from my grandparents' house. There we have all of our friends: the twin girls from next door, our cousin Florin, and lots of others. We have to wear little blue uniforms, learn songs and poems, draw and paint. We learn about the father of all children, Comrade Ceauşescu, and his wife, Elena, the mother of all children and a famous scientist. Their portraits are in our schoolroom; they are always smiling. My favorite days at the kindergarten are at the end of summer when there are sudden rainstorms. The raindrops hit the cement courtyard and bounce up like transparent butterflies, which we sometimes run barefoot to catch. But otherwise I am lazy and get bored easily. Some days I just want to stay home with Bunica, which is never a problem with her. One morning when the kindergarten teacher comes looking for me at the house, Bunica argues with her and sends her back without me: "Mind your own business, dear. Leave the child alone to sleep and play. Life is going to be hard soon enough with real school coming. Ooohhh! You go on now, dear, and have a nice day."

We spend a long time with Bunica holding me and brushing my hair in two long braids, which she ties with red ribbons and flips over my shoulders to my back. She washes my face in the yard with cold water from a tin cup; the water drips all over my toes. She tells me I have hair like Goldilocks, she kisses me, and I love her. She is small, has very soft gray eyes, soft folds of skin on her face, and two thin white braids coiled around her head. Her flowery dresses always go down to her ankles, and her apron, where I like to hide my head when I run to her, smells of parsley.

*

Loredana and I spend the weeks licking cream from the clay pots where Bunica ages milk for buttermilk. We pretend it was the cat that did it, so the cat regularly gets shooed away from the kitchen. We watch the stork come back to her nest on the tall stub of the oak tree in the backyard and fly off with her babes, practicing for migration. We go to the family vineyard with Bunicu to check on the ripeness of the grapes. Bunica is superstitious about everything: if your nose itches on the outside, you will laugh, if it itches on the inside, you will cry; if there is a thunderstorm, it means that Saint Ilie is driving his chariot in the sky and is angry; if you hear the owl at night, you must feed it polenta and salt to send it away with its bad news; if you dream about snakes, next day it will be windy. She has an explanation for absolutely everything, which turns me too into an interpreter of everyone's symptoms and dreams.

The walnuts slowly begin to fall out of the sun-cracked shells on the sidewalk, and we eat lots of seeds straight from the sunflowers, which are as big as my head. Bunica is making prune jam and marmalade over an open fire in the bald part of the yard. The air around the garden smells of burnt sugar and fruit. I hang around waiting for her to dip the wooden spoon in the pot so that I can taste the reddish melted prunes after she stirs them. We are still cooking outside in the backyard at the summer stove. The twig fire crackles and puffs. Loredana and I pick the salads from the garden and wash the tomatoes, while Bunica grills the chicken and rubs it with fresh crushed garlic and sunflower oil garnished with parsley. Bunicu stirs the polenta over the stove, sweating under his black hat. We fry eggs and garnish them with fresh dill, then eat everything with our hands, licking our fingers at the oak table in the garden. The dog begs for bones, now growling at the cat, now making thin throat-sounds for us. About sunset time, the hens climb to their tree to sleep. They flap their brown wings up in the branches, making their *chuckle* sounds as they settle against the trunk.

On Saturday mornings there is the beep-beep of the car at the gates. Out come my parents with oranges, Sibiu salami, candy, and fresh clean clothes for me and my sister. Mom heats up large cauldrons of water for our baths and she scrubs my sister and me, washes our hair, until, satisfied, she declares us "less smelly." After she dresses us, we're ready for a big family lunch. There are tomatoes and dill-stewed white beans with soured pickles and polenta, fresh cheese with bread and roasted or fried chicken served with roasted red peppers dipped in vinegar. We go away with my parents until Sunday afternoon, and just like that the horizon from the window of the room where Bunica, Loredana, and I sleep disappears.

Sometimes we go to the priest's house to visit Grandma Floarea. Dad usually makes an inventory of the materials being brought for building the new house while the rest of us hang around with Bunica. She is quite short, has a sharp voice that carries far into the yard, and for Sunday lunch she cooks us soured meatball soup with polenta. Almost always we bring her a flask of red wine from Bunicu and Bunica, which she loves drinking to get "power" for the work around the house. Bunica Floarea has made friends with all the new neighbors, so there are always ladies coming to visit or already there when we arrive. One of them is Tanti Jana, who wears light green dresses and wraps her headscarf behind instead of tying it under her chin. From a distance, she always smells like wine, and she has happy red cheeks and red hands. Many of the older neighborhood kids help Bunica Floarea with the work around the priest's garden.

By the time our parents drop us back from the weekends with clear instructions to brush our teeth and keep our ears clean, Bunicu and Bunica are already back from church smelling of incense, and Bunicu's hair is all greasy with walnut oil. My sister and I bolt out the door to our friends before Mom and Dad have a chance to get into the car. We like to play hide-and-seek in the cornfields at our neighbors' houses, and we come back home in the evening tired, our limbs and cheeks crisscrossed with scratches from the leaves of corn.

*

One day Bunicu and I are inside playing with Loredana while Bunica is getting water from the well. Loredana sits on Bunicu's left knee and me on the right one and we play the "game" of our favorite cheek: something we learned from a story Bunica read to us. I kiss Bunicu's right cheek because it's my favorite and I slap Loredana's favorite cheek, which is Bunicu's left. Loredana does the same, in reverse. Bunicu says this is a cruel game and tries to tell us the end of the story, but we are too absorbed in acting the characters. Suddenly there are sharp screams. The neighbors are yelling. We rush outside to find Bunica slumped over the edge of the well while the bull hits her in the ribs with its head.

"Oh God, how did the beast break loose?" screams Bunicu.

People from the street try to reach over the well to beat the bull with sticks. "Hoh, hoh, get the beast, the beast!"

Bunicu rushes over and hits the animal as hard as he can to make it stop. He takes it to the backyard. Women rush with water screaming at Bunica to come to her senses, but she is a weak bundle now despite all the water thrown on her face. I am so scared I scream at the top of my lungs that my *bunica* is dying. The priest is called to pray and open the book to see if she's going to live. He spreads his black crow-like robes around her, chants for a long time, and holds her hand until she comes to her senses.

She doesn't have any broken ribs but from this day onward develops breathing problems (which Mom calls in a serious, mysterious tone "panic attacks") and spends most of the time inside the house. *Bunica* calls these breathing troubles *năduf.* Bunicu takes over milking the cow. Slowly he begins to use the new routine to his advantage in the evenings, when he goes to the wine barrels for a few mugs before and after the milking.

"Ah, Neculai, Neculai, if the barrels weren't so close to the cow's shed, you'd never do the milking. Look at your red cheeks, I can smell you all the way from the porch! Make sure you leave some wine for the holidays."

Bunica scolds him every day but he is always happy and laughing, his blue eyes glimmering guiltily. I am still so scared that Bunica might die from the bull that I spend most of the time with her to make sure she doesn't go to the cows' shed. I also hate the bull, forever. Especially when she says that she has *năduf.*

*

It's winter already. The snow seems to cover our grandparents' house. Icicles hang from the lacy finery of the eaves that Bunicu painted blue in the autumn. When the sun comes out it makes stars of the ice clinging to the kitchen windows. The yellow quinces we keep on the windowsill ripen slowly. When we bake them alongside pumpkins they fill the house with the most sweet and spicy cinnamon smell. Bunicu brings dry grapes, which are hung one by one with rope in the attic: they taste both sour and sweet, and the juice is sticky and thick. The fire burns all day long. First we start it with old vine twigs and the leftover candle stubs from church. Then we feed it with logs or coal until it roars. The coal makes the house smell like farts, so we only use it when Bunicu's back hurts so much he can't chop the wood.

Bunica brings big piles of lamb wool inside the kitchen (which we now use as dayroom and bedroom as well) and sits on the bed, where she spins the puffy bits into yarn that I roll over a ball made of newspaper into larger balls ready for dyeing or knitting. The sound of the distaff and spindle twirling is punctuated by her spitting between her right thumb and her right forefinger. Women neighbors come to visit and bring their own knitting or spinning. Most of the time I nap behind Bunica's back or at her side, listening to the stories and gossip from around the village: someone is buying a good cow, someone is selling really good wine from their house, there was a big fight between the neighbors, and so on. The sound of the spinning twirls in the air with a continuous hypnotizing *whirrr.* Bunica used to be the village midwife, so there are many stories of births and first baby baths, of beautiful children and of skinny children or of fat children with hair on their heads already. She says that when babies smile in their sleep it is because Saint Mary looks at them and talks to them.

But she is most proud of Bunicu's midwifery story, which she tells so often I know it by heart. One late afternoon in the autumn (long before I was born) Bunicu was coming home with his cart and horse from the fields. As he passed the edge of the woods where the fields ended, he heard a woman cry near a bush. He stopped the horse and went to see if she had fallen but discovered that her water had broken and she was screaming from birthing pains. He rolled up his sleeves and washed his hands with the drinking water from his bottle, grabbed the sackcloth from the cart, placed it under the woman, and helped her give birth. He held her hands, told her when the head came out, and cleaned the baby's nose. Then he loaded them all in the cart and took the woman to her house, where the doctor was called at the same time as Bunica. When he got home he was covered in blood and was crying with happiness. I am most proud of this story too, because Bunicu is a shy man when it comes to women's stories. I know this because when women talk about children-making, he always leaves the room.

In the evenings, after our dinner of polenta with pork soup soured with lemon salt, Bunicu begins his favorite pastime, which is selling wine by the glass or the bottle to the village folk. Usually five or six people come to the house. They sit around the table talking about their work with the animals or make plans for planting corn and water-melons in the spring. The kitchen becomes an evening sitting room. Loredana and I sit on Bunica's bed with her. Above the bed there is a wall-sized tapestry with Turkish dancers who sound bells that hang from their wrists and ankles. The pink and blue folds of their dresses move below their hips, and around them there are people who sit in a circle, clapping. Loredana and I make up stories about everyone in the tapestry, name the characters, and disagree about who the most beautiful dancer is.

Everyone has tapestries like this around their houses, but ours, with time, stirs my interest in stories about faraway lands, making me a per-fect ear for *One Thousand and One Nights* when I reach preadolescence. So we are all set for guests and stories in the evenings. Bunicu gets a little tipsy, which is my favorite, because he convinces everyone to sing. He asks me and my sister to sing too. The best part is when our neighbor brings his accordion and we stay up really late listening to him play while the rest of the guests tap their feet on the floor gently between sips of wine. I look at the black and white keys dipping under his fingers, coaxing slow sad songs out of the stretching box: it's like watching the chicks peck their way out of the eggs, this seamless and astonished music coming from the man's fingers. It's like a road with different sounds on it, which you discover as you walk along. "*Mină caii*, Neculai," I want to say when the music begins. Many times I fall asleep listening to the songs, as I fall asleep rocked gently by Bunicu's cart moving slowly up the hill on the dirt road.

Holidays

Bunica is cleaning the house with her sleeves rolled all the way up above her elbows. She changes the rugs in the dining room and living room. She also prepares the big foot-treadle loom for after Christmas, when she will set to making tapestries for walls, bedspreads, and rugs from wool and torn clothes in which we no longer fit. She loads the shuttle with colorful yarn and checks the foot pedals to see if they move all the four layers of fabric that she will weave. The gigantic loom takes up most of the space in the *iatac*, which is formally the guest room into which no one goes. She also keeps her crochet work and her Singer sewing machine there. And she cleans and dusts everything in the kitchen, preparing especially the big wooden pestle with which we will grind spices and nuts.

At the weekends Mom brings home rum essence, vanilla, raisins, Turkish delight, and oranges from which we make zest. I crush walnuts and eat more than I save. Bunicu sifts white flour carefully and cleans the big wooden tub where the women from the neighborhood will knead the dough for *cozonac*, the best sweet bread in the world. We make it twice a year, at Christmas and at Easter. The difference is that at Easter we bake the *cozonac* in the clay oven in the yard, which is so big you have to fire it for days and you have to crawl into it, whereas at Christmas we bake everything inside. But there are still three weeks until Christmas. We are beginning to rehearse carols and dances. At bedtime, when Bunica is all mine and my sister's, she tells us the story of the birth of Jesus. Bunicu cuts a fistful of hair from the horse's tail and stretches it with his hands until it looks like a violin bow. He dampens the hair with vinegar and makes a Christmas musical instrument called a *buhai* that is like a drum made with sheepskin to which the horse's hair is sewn. When you pull on the wet hair, the container, usually a bucket to which the skin is attached and stretched firmly, makes a *moo-hhhoo-oohh* sound. You play the *buhai* while others crack whips and ring bells to accompany the carol singers when they banish the old year and welcome the new one.

When the house is all clean, we polish all the icons (especially the one in the kitchen with Saint George fighting the dragon), glue stars made of red foil on the windows, and decorate the Christmas tree in the front room. Then the priest comes to bless the house with basil and holy water. Bunica prepares *turtele de Crăciun*, cakes made with thin layers of unleavened bread grilled over the flat iron stove and moistened with honey and rose water, and sprinkled with cocoa, walnuts, and sugar. She washes and dresses my sister and me properly so that we're all ready for the visit.

The priest makes rounds from house to house in his long black robes, holding his holy book, censer, and cross close to his chest. Usually people wait for him at the gates, trying to look serious and sinless. He comes with his cantor, who has one leg shorter than the other and hobbles about him singing at the top of his lungs. After we kneel before him and the prayers are done, he shakes the basil plant soaked in holy water over our faces and over all the corners of the house. Bunica offers him and the cantor a glass of wine and some *turte*, and she asks me to put some money in their pockets. Needless to say, the priest is always tipsy by the time he arrives back at his house (which is one door down from my kindergarten, making it four doors down from Bunica's house) and we always laugh watching him stumble on the sidewalk. "Hooooh, hoo, HOP! Father," giggles Bunica.

*

The week before Christmas we slaughter the pig, which is the main meat during the holidays. There usually is one pig for all the relatives so the yard comes alive with the family of Aunt Săftica, who is the natural daughter of Bunicu and Bunica. The men bring a pile of hay in the middle of the front yard first. It's cold outside, so there is a bottle of *țuică* (plum brandy made by Bunicu) to go around from man to man. They also fill a big wooden tub with water and sharpen knives on a special round stone. My sister, our cousins, and I are not allowed to watch the killing, which is done by quickly cutting the pig's throat with a hatchet, but we hear the death sounds of the animal and cry. When the pig is ready, the women rush outside with the kids. My cousin Florin, Loredana, and I are lifted onto its back and we ride it like cowboys while people prepare the fire, over which they roll it after they gut it, roasting the skin lightly. Then we rub the skin with coarse salt and clear the pig hair away. Florin, Loredana, and I use sharp sticks to stab bits of pig skin and roast it over the fire till it's nicely burned and the fat drips. We eat the pig skin with raw garlic and the adults wash it down with small sips of red wine. Everyone talks loudly, flushed with *țuică* and the wine. After that, a big meal of grilled or roast meat is served with polenta, potatoes fried in sunflower oil, pickled cucumbers, and pickled watermelons, which are sweet and sour at the same time. At the end of the day, the meat is divided among the families and women start making sausages. Bunica flavors her sausages with so much chili and fresh garlic that you need a whole lot of polenta to eat one little piece without setting your mouth on fire.

Three days before Christmas the carolers come from morning till night. Some of them are dressed in colorful traditional costumes made of white cotton embroidered with flowers and shiny beads, from our part of Moldavia. Women wear special skirts, beaded and layered, and men wear white trousers. Everyone wears thick vests in which all the colors, especially bright red, are woven. The first day they carry the icon of Saint Mary, the second, decorated pine branches. Their songs slip from religious carols to secular Christmas tunes. You can hear their *heee, hoooo,* their bells and laughter way down the road.

The night before Christmas the tree is lit, the carolers dwindle away, and we sit over the last bits of a feast—vine leaves stuffed with rice, meat, and herbs; chicken salad with homemade mayonnaise; sour soup served with soured cream on top; roast pork; polenta; sweet cheese pie; and *cozonac.* The dogs bark so loudly they interrupt our noise. All of our relatives are here; we don't expect any more guests. Mom sends me and my sister to the door to see who it is.

Out in the snow there is *Moş Crăciun* (Santa Claus), who says he's just come from the North Pole to see if there is a Carmen and a Loredana in this house, because he has a sled filled with presents. My sister and I hold each other's hands and jump and squeal, screaming for Mom to come let Santa in. He wears a red cloak and has a huge walking stick decorated with gold ribbons. His face is covered with a mask showing pink cheeks and a long white beard, which we try to pull at. Santa asks us, Bunicu, and Bunica, if we've been good girls. We shout that we were the *best* girls and he begins giving us toys: a multicolored train with tracks, a trivia game with little lights that turn on when you press on the correct answer (it asks you which is the longest bridge in the world and what the capital of Albania is), lots of candy wrapped in colorful foil, new dresses and shoes. My sister and I sing between unwrapping the gifts, we hug Santa and kiss his mask. When he says that his dogs and sled are waiting for him at the gates, we wish him fun with all the other children and go back to our presents. My heart explodes with happiness and colors.

*

Time blinks over melting snow. Heads of snowdrops come out of the surprised warmed earth. *"Zambile albastre"* says Bunica, pointing at the new hyacinth bells in the young grass around the porch. *"Lăcrimioare, zambile albe."* She recites the names like prayers to me, and my child-tongue rolls over the *b*'s and slips over the *a*'s as if I am tasting rose water for the first time. I feel a kind of love for the names of flowers. There is a whoosh of wings above the yard, and Bunica says the migratory birds will return soon. "What's *migratoare?*" I ask, weighing the word in my throat.

"It's when you're the stork homesick for the stub of the oak tree in our backyard and you come home to rebuild your nest."

"Dor de casă," I repeat, looking at her eyes.

And she sings to me the song of the cuckoo bird from Lugoj who left his village and spent all his life singing about it from all the roofs of the world, not taking food or water from kind strangers because he was "sick" with "home." So we wait together for the birds to come home and be healed. I am afraid I will be the cuckoo bird from Lugoj and I hug her around her soft belly.

Suddenly it's Easter Eve. The house smells of baked sweet breads, oven-roasted lamb, and stuffed roasted turkey. Colorful eggs sit in wooden bowls on the tables. Some windows are slightly open and you can feel the still-cold-but-warming breeze in the air. We must go to bed on a light vegan dinner and wait for the midnight bells to call us to the church. This year, because I am almost six and Loredana almost five, my grandparents take us to the midnight service to celebrate the Resurrection of Christ. Just as I fall asleep, it seems, Bunicu and Bunica turn on the lights and shuffle around the house. They dress in new clothes—dark clothes for tonight, as tomorrow everyone will wear bright dresses and shirts. Loredana and I are blind with sleep but wake up when Bunicu gives us each candles decorated with tiny white ribbons and lots of pink, red, and blue flowers. "For the Resurrection," he explains.

The four of us walk out of the house slowly, leaving only one light on in the kitchen to wait for our return. The village is filled with sleepy "good evening to you" greetings. From every street people come out into midnight like a whispering river, looking up at the stars in the clear sky. Everyone whispers. The church bells toll. From the entrance, even the stern saints in the Byzantine paintings look happy to see us. The priest and his helpers are dressed in magnificent regal clothes of gold, violet, and silver, and the priest holds a tall white candle from which fresh spring flowers trail and spill over his hands. There is a small light in the church and he sings, *"Veniți să luați lumină."* My

grandparents take us to the priest's candle and we light ours from it.
I don't know what I feel, maybe a sensation that I am suddenly far
inside Time. There are tears streaming from my face. This is the first
time in my life when collective emotion, a sort of light, pulses through
me and I understand that something bigger than me is happening—
some kind of unity. Everyone smiles. And then hundreds of candles
are lit. The service goes on forever. I fall asleep on each of my grandparents. My sister falls asleep on them too, until we are being pushed
gently in front of the priest to take Communion, when we sing *Hristos
a Înviat:* "Christ Has Risen."

We walk home with our candles still lit, as does everyone else. In
daybreak our tiny lights, which flicker in the wind, are the stars on
earth returning to their beds to sleep. At home Bunica places a red egg
and a coin in a cup, one for each of us, and fills the cup with water.
She asks us to wash our hands and faces with the water for good luck,
and then we sit at the table to eat our boiled eggs. We all keep our
Easter coin. We go to bed as the birds wake up on Easter Day. I fall
asleep holding Loredana's hand, vestments of gold and purple twirling in candlelight in my mind's eye.

*

It's 1976. I turned six this summer. One day, as I play around with my
friends in the trees, the primary school teacher comes and asks me if
I want some of her sunflower seeds. She is fat and short, like a barrel,
and her face is kindly, round, framed by curly short black hair. She
asks me my age and then says, "You know, at school, there are many
children your age who are learning how to read and write. We play
a lot and learn many songs. Do you think you want to join us in the
autumn?"

"*Da?*" I reply curiously as I continue to pick at her sunflower.

It's September 15. My mother looks pretty with a dark short dress
and her long brown hair brushed over her shoulders. I have a leather
bag, a blue uniform: a sleeveless dark blue dress on top of a light-blue
shirt with a white collar. Around the collar Mom has placed a red scarf

hemmed with the Romanian flag: soon I will belong to the Communist Party's Pioneers, just like all of the other children. My hair is brushed in two huge ponytails tied with white bows that look like butter-flies. My beautiful mom holds my hand, crying all the way to school. Her high-heeled shoes make a sharp *clink-clink* on the sidewalk. As we pass by, other kids who will soon become my friends—Aurelia, Mihaela, Mihăiță, Ionica—join us with their moms, who are not as pretty as mine. I don't understand why Mom still cries but she says, "It's an important event. It's your first day of school."

I don't understand the explanation. At school, my teacher is friendly with all of us. After the *careu,* the assembly in the courtyard where we all salute the flag and sing the national anthem, she teaches us a song called "The Little Scholar." She shows us the portrait of Comrade Ceaușescu on the wall. When I come home, Mom is waiting for me at Bunica's well, and she cries again as I sing the song to her. Bunicu and Bunica kiss me, laughing, and Loredana pulls at my uniform, saying, "Me too, next year!"

The House of Straw

It's not quite cold yet. The walnuts are dropping from the trees again and we have finished harvesting the freckled beans, which are now spread in little piles on cotton sheets in the sun. Loredana and I play in the walnut tree. When we crush the green shells from around the nuts, our hands turn yellow and smell of iodine. She and I are together so much that many times we don't really notice each other. Today we are both Tarzan.

Bunicu arrives with his cart from shopping in town. "*Brrrr, brrrr,* Steluța," he says to the horse, which halts by the well. He unloads a few new straw rugs on the grass, and a bag filled with new clothes, a suit for himself complete with shoes, socks, and underclothes, a dress and headscarf for Bunica, as well as a slip and shoes. My grandparents draw a square on the ground and stake pegs at its corners. When the first square is made, they make another, all on the bald part of the front yard, which Bunica swept in the afternoon with a willow broom and sprinkled with water, spread in the shape of arches, to keep the dust down. They are building two rooms with walls of straw rugs, stitched together with wooden pegs. Loredana and I come down from the tree: "Bunicu, Bunica, what are you doing?"

"We're building the houses for our next lives," Bunica answers.

"What's that?" we ask.

As we help, loading each room with a table, chairs, a bed dressed with new white cotton sheets, new quilts, and soft pillows over fresh hay mattresses, they explain to us what they are doing.

"When we die and God takes us to heaven, we must have a house to live in. We get to choose what we want to have in the house. This is why we are putting all these things inside now. But we have to give this house away to poor people first, and then in heaven God gives it back to us as we give it to others now. We call this ritual *grijirea*, and one day it will be your turn to do it. Come help, the priest will be here soon to bless our houses."

In each room we place a fresh set of clothes, slippers and shoes, sacks of grain, rice, and corn. Bunicu, at the last minute, goes to the cellar and gets a flask of wine for his table.

I don't want my grandparents to die, so when the priest arrives with his censer, his holy water, and his twigs of basil, I start crying. I don't stop until Bunica tells me that she will die a very long time from now when she will be so helpless she will be like a baby that I will have to take care of. This seems so far away now that I feel much better.

But I ask Bunica, "You mean when we die, we die like the baby chicken in the spring?"

"Yes, something like that."

In the spring, when Bunica said it was happening, I went to look at the chicks peck their way out of the eggs. Sometimes the hens help the chicks come out by pecking at the shell, softly, from the outside. We bring the baby chickens inside at night (as we always do with a newborn calf or lamb), and during the days we take them out in the sun. This particular day one of the puffy yellow baby chicks stumbled and kept falling over. I called Bunica outside to help me help the chick to its feet. We checked to see if maybe it was choking from grain, or maybe it wanted water, but there was nothing in its mouth. I held its tiny beak open while Bunica put drops of water down its throat. Nothing helped. We watched it jump from one side to another, trying to stand on its feet and falling again. Bunica said, "He is seeing Death now, who came to take him, and he is scared of dying. This is why he tries so hard to run away."

"But what does Death look like?" I asked.

"It's an old toothless hag with a scythe and she takes whoever she wants, in any place she wants."

"Do you think he sees her now"?

"Yes."

"I can get a stick and beat Death up, because I want the chick to live."

"Yes, but you can't see it, so you can't send it away."

I spent the next while crying and trying really hard to imagine Death because I wanted to send it away. When the eyes of the chick whitened over with a curtainlike glaze, Bunica said that Death took him and he had gone to heaven. I held him in my palm until his little chest stopped moving altogether and the whole body went stiff, with the neck stretched out like a wire. We had a funeral for him: made a hole by the quince tree, a cross from sticks, and had lunch. I was afraid of the convulsions the chick endured fighting with the toothless hag. So I say to Bunica, "But you won't convulse like the baby chick before you die, all right?"

"I promise" she says.

When the poor people come to receive their houses of straw from my grandparents, Bunicu and Bunica light candles and say to them, "In this life this house shall be yours and in the afterlife it shall be mine." And they say back, *"Vodaproste."* When all the goods are loaded back into the cart, Bunicu transports them to their new homes and then we have a feast with the neighbors, the poor people, and the priest. Bunica serves homemade cheese with her bread, rice pilaf and roast chicken, stuffed vine leaves and lots of wine. I record this giving-of-the-house ritual in my mind: *grijirea*, it means "caring worry." I am six years old and I will never forget it. Bunica tells me that when she dies, if I want to feel close to her I should light a candle and then buy a fresh bagel and give it away to someone who is hungry; this way she will eat the bagel in heaven and will thank me in dreams. And the hungry person will be full. I swear to do this if she ever dies but I make a correction: her favorite food is sliced potatoes fried in sunflower oil and served with crushed garlic in a little water and garnished with parsley. So I tell her that bagels are fine with me, but I will make sure she also gets her potatoes in heaven. When she kisses me, her tears spill on my cheek.

Earthquake

It's March 1977 and we've just gone to sleep in the kitchen, me with Loredana and Bunica in her bed and Bunicu in his bed. The house is quiet save for the purring of the cat on the chair next to the stove. On the red-brownish cupboard are the washed plates left to dry. All the glasses are back on the shelf. The leftover polenta is covered with a white cloth in the middle of the table, on its wooden cutting board. A half-full bottle of wine stands by the polenta, next to the salt and pepper shakers. Suddenly the bed shakes. The cat jumps into the bed. Outside the dog stirs and barks. Again the beds begin shaking, the radio falls from its small table, the plates crash to the floor, and the bottle of wine rolls on the table, falling to the ground. The walls shake, the cow moos, and the glasses clink in the cupboard. Bunicu tries to get out of the bed but falls back into it. Everyone screams. The earthquake shakes the windows. I sense the ground underneath the bed move. For the first time I understand that the earth is weak and can slip from under me. I will have this feeling many times in my life but such is the order of things that now I am preparing for it without knowing. We hear the neighbors scream.

The epicenter is in Vrancea, where my sister and I were born. I was nearly born on the motorcycle on the way back from a trip my parents took one June day. Since then they have been calling me "the road-child" or "the motorcycle-child." They call my sister "the little Gypsy" because her skin is darker, and my brother, who is not born yet, will be called "the watermelon-boy" because he will be conceived the summer my parents will try their luck raising watermelons on a rented piece of land. Vrancea is the most seismically active region of România and famous in Europe for generating earthquakes. When I hear that the earthquake began in Vrancea, I imagine my birthplace, Nănești, fallen into a dark hole. I am glad we are with my grandparents.

Sometime later, around midnight, Mom and Dad arrive from Ivești. The car beeps to a halt by the well and they rush inside to check on us. There is lots of commotion. The house is standing just fine but the animals are scared, restless. Dad turns on the radio, which announces that the earthquake hit București the worst, with many buildings having collapsed, killing thousands of people. People are urged to stay put till the morning. We meet with the neighbors in the yard and everyone talks about the shaking. Mom and Dad go to check on all our relatives and don't return until the morning, when Dad connects Bunicu's television to the antenna and we see the devastation in București. The next few weeks are a blur of news: people dead, dying, discovered by dogs in the rubble. We are happy to be alive and well. Dad and Mom have puffy eyes from lack of sleep. They keep saying they are sorry we were not all together when the shaking occurred.

*

After the earthquake my parents slow down with planning their new house and we spend the weekends with them in Ivești, or taking small trips to the mountains where we visit castles, old churches, and buy artisan toys. Up the mountain roads, which look like coiled white snakes, we buy cheese stored in cones made of pine wood from locals who have small kiosks at the scenic viewpoints. I love being in the car with Dad, who wears hats all the time, like Bunicu, and smokes cigarettes with the window down. My sister and I chase each other along the stone steps of castles, study the giant statues of women or men dressed in traditional costumes that stand in mountain fields like visions from fairy tales. We barely reach the knees of the statues. Dad asks us to memorize the names of rivers as we cross them. We grill sausages at the picnic stops high up by the fir trees, keeping an eye open for *floarea de colţ,* Mom's favorite mountain flower. The backseat of the car is always filled with ferns and pine cones, making everything smell like vacation.

Sundays are homework days. From three to five, my sister and I have to sit at the table either in Iveşti (where we hate it because we're never there enough to know the place well) or in the kitchen at Bunica and Bunicu's. Mom watches us solve math problems, practice reading, and write sentences in neat calligraphy. The worst bit of it is that we must show my parents the grades we earned during the week, and anything less than a nine out of ten is trouble. Mom lectures us, yells at us, promises to show our low grades to the neighbors to embarrass us for our laziness, and she ends up pulling our ears plenty of times too. Then we have to read our textbooks to her. My problem with reading is that though I know how to read perfectly well, I get bored with the stories I must read from the schoolbook and I invent side action. Mom sees me doing this all the time and asks, "Where did you see this sentence? Why are you inventing stuff? You must be disciplined!"

We argue a lot. If there is a story with a boy named Ionel in the first sentence and the second sentence starts with "One day, Ionel . . . ," then I take the lead, setting him on some adventures like in the Brothers Grimm or ones I imagine entirely by myself. In all my stories the main characters have a secret object that helps them disappear and appear at any time or place they choose, meaning that they can evade anything that has to do with structure and are able to scare or to make happy anyone in the story. This making up stuff certainly gets me lower grades in school but I also notice that my teacher and my classmates really like what I make up, especially because my main characters seem to know everything before anyone else. So I don't see the point of discipline.

Bunica sticks to my side of the argument: "The girl must develop her mind. Leave her alone. There is going to be enough reality soon enough!"

When Dad takes over it's because he teaches us the clock, the multiplication tables, and chess. He is annoying because Bunicu and Bunica have already taught us how to read the clock and the multiplication table when we were in kindergarten but he never noticed. Now we're playing chess, which is fun in some ways (especially making the horses hop in an L shape), but the boring part is that every single Sunday afternoon we have to watch the chess masters *(Şah-Mat)* television program, where moves are explained. Then we have to try to imitate them. Every time my dad wins I cry with frustration. He not only celebrates his wins, he gloats.

The Black Sea

It is the June of my seventh birthday and school is out. Mom and Dad are going to make up for all the weekend discipline and boredom by taking us on a long vacation to the Black Sea—in only a few weeks! I don't remember the other times we went because my sister and I were too small, but this time we are very excited. We have brand-new blue beach towels, toys, bathing suits.

The night before we leave we hardly sleep, and when we get into the car it's still dark outside. Bunica asks me to bring her seashells. Then she whispers to me, "Tell me if the sea is really black. Will you remember this?"

I remember.

At Mamaia the sand is crackly and golden. The waves are so big they go up to Dad's chest. As far as you can see it's blue: the sky, the sea, the horizon, waves chasing each other in the sand. The sea is never-ending, ever-changing hues between blue and green, all except the foamy white crests of the waves. Dad takes us to see the sunrise on the beach: the sun comes out of the water, an incandescent ball. He chases us and Mom in the salty, chilly breeze, close to the noisy waves on the tide-wet sand. We buy lots of toy tools to make sand castles, eat fresh peaches every day after lunch. There are boats and safari-like settings in the parks with lions and elephants and we find the seven dwarfs too, all made of plastic. My sister and I wear mariner's dresses and blue-tinted sunglasses. We pose with all the creatures and climb into all the boats that go nowhere. But the true source of fun is Dad.

He takes us up on his shoulders and throws us into the sea, making Mom scream with worry. He has strong shoulders and arms. We climb on his back, asking him to swim far out with us. Mom is best at jumping waves: we hold hands while we wait for the wave to lift us and jump on it at the last minute so that for a few seconds our bodies crest with it toward the shore. The sea shows us starfish, and fish that Mom and Dad hunt with forks in the rock crevices. The tides come all the way to the restaurant terrace, making the chairs dance. Our favorite resort is called Vraja Mării, the Spell of the Sea. There is music everywhere. My sister and I are in the happiest dream. In the evenings, when Mom cooks at the small gas stove on the beach, Polish and East German tourists sell black-market clothes, tents, and sleeping bags from the back of their cars. We make friends with them in sign language mostly and offer them Bunicu's *țuică* before we buy stuff from them. Mom checks her weight on all the scales, complaining that she is getting fatter, but honestly I think she is beautiful in her red bathing suit.

One day we take a small white sailboat to Ovid's island, in the middle of a lake on the other side of the sea. Dad and Mom tell us about the poet's exile from Rome and how in the end he made friends with the fishermen, so he wasn't that sad in his exile after all. My imagination rushes with the idea that someone had to be away from his homeland forever. I cannot see how it would be possible for me to stay alive without Bunicu, Bunica, Steluța the horse, and all the rooms in their house with their maze of doors like the priest's house. The story reminds me of the cuckoo bird from Lugoj. The boat swishes over water. The water is shimmering bluish milk: "pearly," my mother says. I am rapt from the stillness of the lake, the sunset, the wind in the sail. I feel as if I am going far away in a world suspended between the heavens and the earth. On the island we drink lemonade with straws and eat polenta with roast chicken, not nearly as good as Bunica's, something I remember to tell her as soon as we're back home. And I bring her a plastic bag crammed with shells, which she smells and arranges in a dish with the sand I give her. "The sea is blue blue blue, Bunica, only the name is black."

The Angels in Bunica's Dream

Our grapes have turned purple-plum-red. The frost covered the ground last night for the first time but the days are warm and smell of ripeness. If this were a concert piece, I would say this is the day of the violin breathing its deepest and clearest notes. It's afternoon now. There is a strong breeze, which helps Bunicu sift the beans from the husk. When he pours them from the bucket lifted above his head, the wind takes hold of the husks and blows them in a dry noisy cloud over the bald part of the yard. I have a sense of being lost in a crowd of butterflies. The beans shine like fat raindrops as they fall in piles on the cotton sack.

Bunica brings out a loaf of bread she baked in the morning. "How about we try some of the grapes now with this bread?"

Bunicu sets down his work. We all collect big juicy grapes that hang near the porch, where they grow over a tunnel-like frame. Bunicu takes his scissors and cuts them carefully from the vine; Bunica washes them in a white basin. Loredana and I sit opposite Bunicu and Bunica at the oak table in the grassy side of the garden, in the shade. The taste of the grapes is sweet and sharp; it bites my mouth just slightly and the bread soaks up the juice, making each bite taste fresh like happiness. Bunica loves grapes, so she eats very slowly, really tasting them.

Then she says, "Neculai, I got *năduf.*" All of a sudden, her head drops with a bang onto the table next to the bread and the grapes.

"Anghelina, what on earth are you doing? Is this a joke?" Bunicu asks in panic. But she convulses like the chick that died in the spring and words come out in stutters, squeezed between her face and the table. We don't know what she is saying. Bunicu tries to lift her head but she keeps convulsing. The blue flowers on her printed dress shiver on her back. One cheek now has moved higher than the other and she can scarcely breathe.

"Anghelina, Anghelina, Anghelina!!!!"

"Bunica, bunica, bunicuța mea, bunicuța mea, bunica mea," my sister and I scream. She cannot answer. I cannot breathe either. Loredana has turned purple-red from screaming. We run away from the table yelling for help, for the neighbors to come. Bunica has had a severe stroke.

"Bunicuța mea, bunicuța mea," Loredana and I call out, shivering. "Please come back to us, please come back to us."

Eventually the doctor comes, and the priest, and my parents, and half the village crowd around the yard. The only one I trust is the priest, who makes circles around her with the censer, anoints her with holy oil, blesses her with basil and holy water, and opens the book: "Take heart," he says. "Anghelina will live, the book has opened on the red writing."

Mom and Dad take Bunica to the hospital for about a week, after which she returns home not quite recognizable. She goes into a coma from which she doesn't wake up for about thirty days. Mom is here all the time with Dad, squeezing drops of water in her mouth, washing her, changing the bed. I go to school every day holding Loredana's hand and we talk about the chick that died in the spring, about Death, the toothless hag coming after our *bunica*. We return straight home to her. We don't play anymore. Bunica shrinks in bed into a much smaller version of herself.

And then, one day, just like that she wakes up from her coma and says she is a little hungry. Mom and Tanti Săftica call the priest again, thinking she is now really going to die. But she speaks very slowly, in strange mangled words. She had a dream that she was walking around heaven in fields of fresh clean grass. There was a small congregation of angels with pink and blue robes all hemmed in gold silk. The angels

Bunicu Neculai
(Neculai Butnaru)
in Drăgăneşti,
with his cart and
horses. Steluţa is
on the right.

Bunica Anghelina
at her funeral

Mom at her desk in Iveşti,
at the grocery store with
her helpers

Carmen and Loredana
at their first
kindergarten show

Mom, Dad, Carmen,
and Loredana at
the Black Sea

Loredana and
Dad playing
on the porch of
our new house

Mom, Carmen,
and Loredana
with statue
showing
traditional
costume

Carmen, age seven

Carmen and
Loredana as
"pioneers"

Cătălin in
the hospital
in Bucureşti

Family's arrival at the Grand Rapids, Michigan, airport, November 17, 1989. From left to right: Dad, Paul Stover (the minister of the church that sponsored us), Loredana, Mom, Carmen

Family at American citizenship ceremony, Gerald Ford Museum, Grand Rapids Michigan, 1995. From left to right: Carmen, Cătălin, Dad, Mom, Loredana

had kind faces, gold halos dancing around their young beautiful heads, and they had stork wings. They fed her big plates of *sărmaluțe*, polenta, pilaf, and baked chicken. And for dessert they gave her many sweet cheesecakes. It never rained in heaven, but there was always the most beautiful warm breeze that brought with it angels' music like the choir at the church. This music took her to a place of peace and no pain. Bunicu, Tanti Săftica, Mom, and Dad say she is hallucinating. The priest says God takes care of the good souls, here's the example: she is a holy woman. Bunicu offers the priest a glass of wine, sighing, "Mind you, Father, God could have been a bit easier on us, the children being scared with the stroke and everything."

Me, I believe each and every word she says. I also believe she will live longer because she is too good for the hag with the scythe, whom I try really hard to imagine so I can beat her up. And she does live, until I am ten, but now we must move back with my parents and divide our time between Bunica Floarea at the priest's house and Ivești. As every child knows, I know that the never-ending days of happiness will vanish once my sister and I are out of this house.

Pouring the Foundation

At school we are punished a lot—corporal punishment. Everyone, including our parents, believes that a good beating cultivates discipline. Each teacher has a preferred method of disciplining us, and there are plenty of rules that we seem to break. If the sleeves of your uniform are not perfectly white, if you have dust under your nails, if your homework is full of mistakes, if your ears are dirty, or if you whisper to your friends while the teacher gives the lesson, then you are punished. Sometimes, to teach us the meaning of community, the whole class gets a beating if one child is naughty. The most common "method of discipline" is the ruler: you must extend your palms in front of you and wait for the teacher to hit them with the wooden ruler. The pain is so sharp it makes you want to pee, so immediately after the slap we all grab the iron bars that support the desk chairs to cool off the sting. I dread these regular punishments so much, I seem to forget things as they are happening, except for the funny ones, of course. Children's skin has a short memory, I know this from Bunica Floarea, who often says, "By tomorrow you won't remember a thing, plus a little beating makes you grow stronger."

By that logic, I will grow a large behind, extremely long palms, and very fat cheeks, for this is where everyone beats me. My elementary teacher is the same one Mom had. When she scolds me for my inefficiency or incompetence, she gets so close to my face her spit sprays all over my cheeks and her eyes seem to take up all of her face. "Watch out for the *precipitation*," my sister teases me.

When I was in the first grade, before Bunica Anghelina had the stroke she sometimes allowed me to stay home to get away from this one teacher, just like she did when I was in kindergarten. The teacher came to the house looking for me and I hid under the bed. She got on her hands and knees and pulled me (and the cat) from under the bed, covered in spider nets. After that I never missed school.

But it's the French teacher, a fashionable woman of thirty or so, still unmarried (which is scandalous), who breaks the Romanian flag when she hits my bottom with it because I haven't memorized the conjugations. Everyone in the class roars with laughter and for a while I am nicknamed *cur de piatră:* stone bum. Mom signs my sister and me up for private French lessons but we only learn children's songs about pretty birds and brother Jacques, and read the stories of *Le Petit Prince*, all useless when it comes to verbs.

If we tend to forget the corporal punishment, we never forget the "stories with a moral purpose" we are told in our classes. The one that bothers me the most is the story of a naughty girl who, with every bad behavior toward her parents, drives a nail into their hearts. As she is eventually overcome by remorse at the sight of her parents' hearts filled with nails, she decides to undo her bad acts by behaving particularly well for a while. But when she manages to take all of the nails out of her parents' hearts, her father tells her, "The nails are gone, but look at all the holes that remain in our hearts." No matter how much Mom and Dad try to comfort me after this story, saying that the wounds heal as well, and rather quickly, I am left with the image of a bleeding heart full of holes, which tortures me every time I feel guilty about being rude to my parents.

*

We must all participate in the forced after-school "volunteer work for pioneers." At the beginning of the second grade, we are given black-and-white uniforms adorned with the red Communist scarf, hemmed with the Romanian flag. At the ceremony we are told all about becoming responsible citizens who help our party with agricultural work, recycling, and whitewashing the tree trunks along the streets so that the worms do not destroy their leaves. We are promised medals both for our community work and for distinguishing ourselves in learning. Soon my friends and I are terribly competitive, all aiming to collect the most medals for community work, leadership, and academic achievements. Competition makes me feel anxious, it makes my stomach hurt and burn, but there is no other way to be at school, where the teachers always bring to the front of the class the most decorated pioneers and tell us that "we must vote them, democratically," as our "leaders" or "class commanders" because they are "better" than the rest of us.

One of the chores is to raise *viermi de mătase* (silkworms) in the spring-summer term. At lunchtime, when classes end, our desks are covered with large white worms like butter beans that grow peanut-shaped shells. They are sticky, soft, and cold to the touch and release this strange worm-and-green-leaves smell all over the classrooms and hallways. We return to school after lunch with plastic bags filled with mulberry leaves, which we spread over the worms only to see them disappear under a climbing frenzy of white. It is fascinating and repulsive in equal measure: I am scared stiff of the worms and the smell makes me nauseated, but at the same time I am drawn to the way they devour the leaves, turning them into moving lace.

Other chores are harvesting the grapes and the tomatoes, and cleaning the school windows; these are reserved for older children who are given grades for the amount of work they perform, which is measured by teachers in school ledgers and then assessed at the end of the school year along with academic grades to determine if we are "good workers." But everyone partakes in the collection of herbs and medicinal flowers. I love picking chamomile flowers, I never think of it as a chore for school, though it is. In the final few weeks of the summer term we have to bring in grocery bags filled with the flowers, which the teachers spread over newspapers to dry. Loredana, our cousin Florin, and I grab our friends from around the neighborhood and go into the fields outside the village. We take the river way, tangling ourselves in the willows, swinging on the branches, skipping stones over the face of the muddy water. We pass by the Gypsy shacks with their dogs, colorful skirts hanging to dry on rope lines between quince trees, and beautiful dark-skinned children with olive eyes. In the great fields we can barely see the last houses of the village. The plains are so flat that the smallest hill looks like a wave begging to be climbed. Chamomile flowers are everywhere, making the fields fragrant. I love crushing the flowers in my palms to squeeze out the green smell and the flower smell from the yellow bit all at once. We gather flowers until our lips become parched with thirst and then return to our homes on the hot dirt roads feeling like explorers who bring gifts from faraway lands.

*

We are back at the "priest's house" with Bunica Floarea, who supervises the slow digging of the new foundation and also looks after us while Mom and Dad work at Iveşti. The builders, a middle-aged husband-and-wife team from our village, spend most of their time napping behind the sacks of cement. Bunica swears and tries to work in their place. When Loredana and I come from school she is covered in dust.

We haven't yet demolished the priest's house, so we spend lots of time playing at the "spy-window" with our new neighbors, Vasilica, Laura, Liliana, Tia, Florin, and Aurora, who is Laura's cousin and visits her every day. All of them have pitch-black hair but Tia has a smattering of bright blond on the left side of her head that looks strangely like a yellow flower pinned inside her black curls. Laura has dimples that deepen when she laughs. Liliana and Vasilica live in a clay house just across the street from us, but we spend most of the time in their vineyard playing hide-and-seek and eating sour grapes until our stomachs tie up in cramps. Aurora is my favorite because she seems quiet and serious and she likes to sit still for a long time. I want to know what she thinks about when she sits like that on the grass, but she is still new to me so I am a bit shy around her. Our street, made of dirt and grass, has no name, and our houses have no numbers, but

everyone in the village, including the stray dogs, is known to the post-
man. When it rains, puddles appear like moon-seas between the gates
to the houses. There are four wells on our street, each with a fruit tree
next to it. We climb the cherry tree next to the well with a stone bench
and play Tarzan and Jane, eating cherries while the dogs bark at us
from underneath. On hot summer days we drop watermelons down
the well to chill them, then fish them back up with the buckets.

Mom and Dad come home with a violin and a guitar, the violin for
Loredana and the guitar for me. At first they drive us to Tecuci once
a week for lessons from a very old couple, really ancient-looking, with
old-people breath and shuffling slippers made of cotton. Loredana
faces her music stand like a toy soldier pursing her lips, while I sit, my
back stiffened with pain, holding on to the guitar as a shield between
my incompetence and my teacher. His face crumples painfully when I
mute half of the F chord as I pull it from the strings. Mostly I concentrate on holding my farts that make my belly hurt a lot. At the end of
each lesson, homework in hand, we are so relieved to be released that
we kiss the teachers goodbye. Later in the term my parents allow us
to take the bus. When we miss the bus we walk the seven kilometers
home. We get tired and bored carrying our instruments, so we stop,
take them out, and play at the side of the road, singing at the top
of our lungs. I am learning classical guitar along with some Italian
popular songs such as "Santa Lucia." Loredana learns to play George
Enescu and to accompany me. But when we play together, because
we have nothing that resembles a musical ear, we sound like monkeys
banging on wood and pulling at strings. Invariably some of our parents' friends see us on the road from Tecuci to Drăgănești and take us
home, where they joke with Mom that they found two little beggar
kids singing for food.

Around this time I start composing poems. My mother is the one
who listens to them, asks me questions about them, and is impressed
with some of the lines. I am impressed with her being impressed with
me, because clearly she is not particularly hopeful either for my French

or for my guitar performances. When I catch her alone in the kitchen preparing her "bird milk" dessert—egg custard topped with soft meringue and homemade vanilla ice cream—I read her my latest poem about the Black Sea being guarded by the tall, fierce Carpathians. She is not an editor but she is a demanding audience: "Is there anything that rhymes with *marea*?" she asks.

When I try to set my poems to music, well, that's when I lose her interest.

*

On the days when we visit Bunica Anghelina as one big family, we record her speaking about her life. I am nine years old, turning ten. I keep asking my mother what age Bunica is but I always forget it, she is so much older than me. We make lots of tapes with her remembering her childhood, her maiden years, and her marriage. We take turns asking all kinds of questions while Bunicu sits quietly by her bedside with humid eyes and a glass of wine in his hand, mostly lost in memories, I guess. My parents insist on all of us sitting around Bunica and talking with her until she is fast asleep. I remember absolutely nothing of her stories, but her uneven, labored voice moves through me like a slow cart up a dusty road. The syllables slip from one end of her breath to the other to make up broken words about digging the second well at the house or delivering a baby with bright pink cheeks into the arms of a young mother. Tongue-knotted *năduf*.

*

Bunica Floarea is not nearly as gentle or polite as Bunica Anghelina but she is loads more fun. She swears loudly and talks to herself all hours of the day: "Kilometers and kilometers I make in this house every day and no time for a drop of wine. Goddamn hard life, I work like a miner in this place. Kilometers and kilometers." Every rule of "proper use of language" that my mother attempts to inflict on my sister and me is beautifully discarded straightaway. By now my sister and I speak a lot like her. Since my parents are still very authoritarian and Loredana and I become anxious when we see their car turning on our street in the evenings (we recognize our Dacia by the headlights because one is dimmer and more yellow than the other), she also teaches, by her example, how to pretend to obey all the rules and how to break each one of them to our satisfaction.

Bunica Floarea is told every morning not to do any heavy lifting and not to exert herself so much, because she won't be able to demolish the priest's house by herself and build our new one. But she is tired of how slowly things are going and tricks my parents into thinking she isn't breaking her bones working. She keeps a clean blue apron and her black dirty apron hanging on the nail behind the kitchen door. She spends the day carrying heavy building things in the iron wheelbarrow. Most of the time she stumbles under the weight, dangling from side to side, her dress swinging after her thin, shaky legs. As soon as she sees the car approaching the house she runs into the kitchen and switches aprons from black to blue, so it looks as if she hasn't touched any of the garden soil or the heavy bags of cement people bring for mixing mortar that will finally go into the foundations. Bunica Floarea embodies proper living under the severe, overly protective, quick-to-lecture regime of my mother and father. They have no idea she is unbreakable!

*

Bunica Floarea has had a really tough life. During the war she endured famine with all her children, whom she raised by herself.

"Your father," she tells me, "had curly blond hair and beautiful green eyes. When we went to buy bread he would run after me with his shoes slung by laces over his shoulder and he'd eat the corners of the bread loaf on the way home. I'd keep the bread under my armpits but he'd jump like a little pony for it."

Bunicu Toader, her husband, beat her day and night and then abandoned everyone for his lover next door. Bunica got a job after the war selling tickets on local buses and she taught her boys how to raise goats on the outskirts of the village to provide extra food. Probably because of her hard life, she has an extraordinary sense of fairness toward all of her children: when she travels between their homes, she makes sure to perform a redistribution of goods from one family to the next, without ever asking for approval. Mom and Dad call this "pure communism" but cannot argue with her because she yells at them not to be ungrateful for all the things she is trying to put right with the world. So because we have more Spee cleaning detergent than the rest of my dad's relatives, she takes as many packs as she can carry when she goes to make her weekend visiting rounds, and returns to us with pickled cabbage from my dad's sister and goat's cheese from my dad's brother.

*

Every day when my sister and I come home from school, the little blue kitchen smells of sliced fresh potatoes fried in sunflower oil until they are absolutely crispy golden. In a deep bowl we find a small pile of freshly crushed garlic mashed in lots of strong olive oil and dressed with fresh parsley, black pepper, and salt. And on a separate plate there is a ball of bright yellow polenta filled with goat's cheese, melted from the heat. Usually, as we walk in, Bunica Floarea is squeezing lemons for the lemonade. She packs everything carefully in thermoses and plastic bags, tells us to send her greetings to Bunica Anghelina, and sends us on our way. Sometimes Loredana and I eat some of the food on the road and we lie to Bunica Anghelina that the portion happens to be a bit smaller, but most of the time we deliver everything intact. (In any case, it's not worth lying about this because both grandmothers can sense our garlic-reeking breath. Bunica Floarea calls us greedy pigs who eat a dying woman's potatoes and we feel guilty.)

From the priest's house to my grandparents', my sister and I invent chasing games. As always, Loredana is better than me, but she suffers from asthma, which makes her all red and then blue before she comes back again to normal. Mom and Dad have taken her from one specialist to another but the only thing that helps her is to spend time at the spas and in the salt mines, in the mountains. We go to visit her whenever she goes for her cures. She and I make up stories about salt dragons and faces of ghosts we see inside the mines. The walls of the mines are gray-blackish and if you stay inside long enough, your throat tastes salty when you come out. Patients usually have to do some light exercises that help them fill their lungs with the salty air. Sometimes you can find chapels inside the mines with altars made of salt and icons at which patients leave flowers. The one trip I really hate, though, is to the children's hospital that specializes in lung and breathing problems. All the children there look extremely skinny, their blue veins like strings along their necks and arms. The place is quite dirty, the beds are smelly, and when Loredana sees us she cries, begging us to take her home. My parents are shaken; they promise they will never send her to another hospital. And so we start chasing specialist doctors all over the country again. We bring them "little attentions" such as Kent cigarettes and real coffee, along with Bunicu's wine and homemade butter, and lots of money in envelopes, so that they will make an extra effort to treat her. By the time she starts to feel better, we have seen too many doctors to remember their names and know all the health spas in the mountains.

When we bring Bunica Floarea's food, I spend lots of time with Bunica Anghelina telling her stories from school or about the building materials Mom and Dad bring for the new house, and I help her sit up a little to feed her. She asks for lemonade a lot because her medication makes her nauseated, and she also says she gets a lot of *năduf.* Her face is very wrinkled now and her mouth opens only on one side. She is no longer who she was, and there is a heavy air of sadness around her. Loredana checks up on Bunicu Neculai, who is often cleaning the animal stables or working around the yard. I hear them laughing like they are old friends. Bunica Anghelina often touches my cheeks with her weak, dry fingers. She is so gentle and so loving, invisible things melt inside of me. Usually we take home fresh milk from Bunicu's cow and a couple of times a week he also gives us a bottle of "power" for Bunica Floarea, which she drinks slowly with Tanti Jana on the porch.

*

Bunica Anghelina is dying. Our family and our neighbors crowd in the small kitchen taking turns standing and sitting at her bedside. Her breath is slowly going from her legs upward and as they become stiff, the air labors in her middle and upper body. I watch her belly become stiff and her chest heave. I think it takes a long time for the soul to leave the body if you are dying slowly in old age. It is the first time I see anyone die. When Tanti Săftica and Mom know it is happening, they take Loredana and me away to the *iatac* with some neighbors: it is getting late. Tanti Săftica and Mom return to Bunica with lit yellow candles. They say that the soul of the dying person struggles to go out if there is someone in the room who feels too much sympathy, so it lingers to comfort the one who is grieving. This is what happens with my mother and Bunica. I can understand this even at the age of ten: my mother owes her happiness to Bunica and it must be awful for her to let go. Tanti Săftica sends Mom to Loredana and me for the last few minutes and all I know of this is Mom holding both of us in her arms and crying until the sound of keening rises from the kitchen where my *bunica* breathes out her soul—out the window, into the night.

Keening is a ritual that blends weeping with singing, the sonorous with the throat-squeezed, hiccupped farewell. Mourning is a gentle release of pain through a song about eyes turning into bluebells, bones turning into flutes, and the belly growing into a tree. Maybe this is why in many Romanian stories there is someone playing a flute under a tree—souls speaking with each other. Or maybe death really is nothing but an allegory. It is the lot of the women to keen, so in our village there is a choir of them to walk everyone to the cemetery, their song halting in their throats as they weep and swallow the grief, to make it part of themselves. The family women all unbraid their hair and cover it with black scarves. Tanti Săftica, Bunica's oldest daughter, has black-and-silver hair that falls down her back all the way to her hips.

I think that poetry is a little like keening too. The best poems pause on the sob in your throat, weeping both for what is beautiful and for what is lost to darkness and evil. There is, for example, the legend of the master builder Manole, who began building a church that kept crumbling each night, reducing the day's work to nothing. A spirit told him that a sacrifice was needed, so the first wife with a young child who came to feed the workmen next day must be buried in the walls of the building, cemented over by her husband. His own wife was the one who came the next day. With a heavy heart he buried her in the upper walls of the church, which then stood until it was finished. The story says that for days he heard his wife and child weep inside the wall. Sad for his loss, for the sacrifice the building had asked of him, Manole made a set of wings for himself from planks of wood and flew from the top of the church to his death. The legend is told in poetry, in rhymes, and every time I hear it, it sounds like keening to me.

But dying is no more than a transformation, for the legend Miorița, which we all sing and recite from when we are little, speaks of a shepherd seeing himself as a groom when he dies: nature takes part in the wedding ritual by turning fir trees into candles, stars into candlelights. I am not sure exactly where Bunica goes tonight as breath leaves her but she has told me so many times about her house of straw and her heaven that I am desperate to believe her.

*

I wake up to find Bunica laid out in the front room in a coffin brimming with flowers. There is a round candleholder making small burning sounds on the stand at the head of the coffin; thin yellow candles flicker and drip into the sand sprinkled in the silver base. This looks like a constellation at the entrance to the front room, next to the *iatac* where the spindle is laid to rest forever with the Singer sewing machine, and Bunica's slippers forgotten since the autumn when she stopped walking around. Around the coffin there are chairs arranged in a circle. She looks like the sun and we are the planets halted in our turning. For three days and nights the room fills with people coming, leaving, standing, sitting, suffocating the coffin with fresh flowers on top of wilting flowers. The priest has crossed Bunica's hands on her chest and lodged a silver cross between her palms. I invent my own keening song for her because I have my own things to say to her. I only keep the tune. Bunicu replaces the candle stubs, greets people, and sits or stands at her head quietly.

I ask as many children as I can to come home with me for one of the funeral meals (they happen just after the burial, at three days, at nine days, and then at thirty days). I bring home half of the school. Mom and the women rush to set up extra tables and chairs in the yard where Loredana, our cousin Florin, and I eat with our friends. Each plate of food eaten here will arrive in heaven for Bunica as full and as perfect as Mom and Tanti Săftica prepared it for us. I want to make sure that Bunica has plenty of provisions so she can walk around heaven and store them in her house of straw. In a way, this is a celebration, though there are still white and black ribbons tied to the doors and people still bring flowers. The yard is filled with the aroma of continuously cooked meats, rice, polenta, and sweets, and we are all together, the whole big family. I want to observe this tradition, I want to be part of things done in an orderly way.

*

It's the night after the *pomană*, the funeral feast. Bunica visits me in a magnificent dream of thanksgiving. She meets me at the blue gate of heaven in the middle of a green and flowery field with lots of chamomile in it. The field stretches all the way up into the sky and there are angels at the gate. She wears her usual black scarf, a blue cardigan, and her flowery blue dress and she is so happy to see me, her smile is as huge as the moon. We walk hand in hand along a beautiful path crossing over gently rolling hills. All along the road there are plates of food from the funeral meal, steaming and aromatic. There are lit candles here and there too, by the plates. She tells me how she loved the food and how much she loves me and how she will always be with me in dreams. Also she says to tell Mom and Tanti Săftica that they did a great job with the funeral and the cooking. Then she walks me back to the gate. I make my way home. In the morning I tell everyone the dream: it is now a family-owned dream. Something happens to me after the dream: I know about death and about life.

*

We are not trying to forget Bunica's death but are keeping busy. My parents fired the couple of sleeping builders; they have hired a lot of men. Every day now, trucks with cement bricks arrive at the priest's house. The bricks are hollow so Loredana and I make little houses for stray kittens and puppies in the small cement squares. We raise an army of pets while people prepare to pour the foundation for the house. Mom and Dad consult us about which rooms we would like to choose for ourselves. We look at the drawing from the architect and then run along the contours drawn in the earth. I choose the room that will look over the street and the well we will build for ourselves. Loredana chooses the room that will look at the church. We decide we will plant trees all around the house so the place will look like a fantastical jungle. Mom and Dad agree. They show us where the living room will be, the dayroom, the kitchen, the veranda, the bathroom, and the attic. Dad promises a big sky window, so we can play in the attic. My parents look at dreams and build them on the empty ground just like Loredana and I do every day. When we actually pour the first buckets of liquid cement in the outline of the house, in the deep trench, we take turns pouring our hearts in it: I will know for the rest of my life that somewhere on earth my ten-year-old hands poured a foundation with my sister, my mother, and my father, and this mark of life will remain mine as much as my name will always name me, despite the passing of time.

Dad is building his second house, starting from nothing. Before we were born he was imprisoned for protesting against the incoming Communist regime—he was twenty-six years old. I don't know this particular detail yet. My parents started once earlier, when they were first married—from nothing—in Nănești, Vrancea, where Loredana and I were born. The only thing they owned was a motorcycle with a side car that my father really loved. In my first month of life I fell ill with a cold. Mom took me to hospital by ambulance. The word finally got to Dad, who was repairing radios in a nearby village. By the time he arrived at the hospital, I was unresponsive. Mom says he ran into the ward yelling that he wanted to see me. At the sound of his voice I opened my eyes and then I looked straight at him. Dad was so affected by this he said to Mom, "Whatever you do, do not take your eyes off Carmen. I will sell the motorcycle, will sell everything to pay these doctors to take care of her." When I arrived at home, to calm me down and stop me from crying, he put the radio next to the pram where I was sleeping and made a string of colored lights that Mom said I loved to look at. In the end, they said, they decided they were too lonely without our grandparents, so they left everything and moved back to Drăgănești. But it was more than loneliness; it was about informers spying on both of them and about the Securitate, the secret police, making it hard for them to live in Vrancea. This is also something I will learn about later. Now I watch how my father swears and turns red any time Comrade Ceaușescu appears on television or makes radio addresses explaining how România is the strongest, most independent country in the world and how we are all members of the "great socialist dream."

This time Mom sees quince, apple, and cherry trees while Dad sees apricot and peach trees. We have space for all of them and will plant one of each plus some plum trees, dahlias and peonies, tulips, a vegetable garden, roses for preserves, and one big tunnel of grapevines going between the entrance gate all the way to the garage door. We imagine everything. As we build our dreams in the tiny priest's house, at the small wobbly table in the blue kitchen, my sister and I are also becoming the street entertainment: we tell everyone about how our house is going to be and we put on concerts in the evening for our neighbors, using the bricks for the stage, flashlights for stage effect, the violin and the guitar for musical performances, and the dressed-up cats and dogs for our characters, not to mention that all the children in the street are members of the cast with their own roles to perform.

Bunica Floarea cooks for an army of workers every day. Mom and Dad come from Iveşti loaded with food and materials for the house. Bunicu Neculai comes for dinner all the time with his bottles of wine. He is lonely and his eyes are becoming washed out, yet he comes to play with us and on Sundays he arrives smelling of incense and walnut oil, as ever.

*

Tanti Jana drinks wine with Bunica on the porch. I listen to them talk.

"The land is cursed, I tell you," says Tanti Jana.

"Now, what kind of thing is that to say?" asks Bunica, looking as if this is going to be a great nonsensical story.

"The priest and his wife who lived here since I can remember had a young daughter, about fifteen. She roamed around with the boys a lot a couple of years before the priest sold the house. When she was pregnant they kept her mostly inside but we all knew, we all saw her at the well with the big belly. There was no father for the child—it was a flower child—so she killed the child and buried it right here under this apple tree. I tell you, the crows come and sit on this tree screaming the whole time, can't you see the crows? There was murder here, woman, I tell you."

I tell Mom the story as soon as she comes in that evening. I am badly shaken. "Mom, Mom, Tanti Jana told Bunica that our house is cursed, that no good will come of it because the priest's daughter killed her child and buried it under the apple tree right here behind the church!"

But my mother laughs and tells me this is such an unbelievable story, only Tanti Jana can invent it when she drinks a whole bottle of wine. She says we're building *our* house here and it is going to be as beautiful as in the dreams and that the land is blessed with all the things we're going to plant in it. So I stop believing in the stories Tanti Jana tells, with her bright red cheeks and her continuous swearing that she speaks the gospel truth. She is irresistible, though. She seems to know something about everyone and she is such a storyteller, I am stuck to her.

*

Meanwhile, our house is nearly finished. It is fitted with running water, electricity, stoves, furniture, big tapestries with scenes from paintings in all the rooms, Persian rugs in deep crimsons and burned terra-cotta or all kinds of deep blue. Loredana's asthma is getting better. She is stronger and more interested in gymnastics, so we spend lots of time practicing exercises like Nadia Comănici. The priest's house is completely demolished and in its place there is freshly turned earth, which is now the front yard. Mom and Dad are going crazy planting trees and making a small garden for each of us: one for me, one for Loredana, one for them. We choose the trees we like, our favorite perennials, we draw and color in the shape of our gardens. I stay away from the bit of land near the apple tree. I choose to plant a peach tree and an apricot tree, one with the help of Mom and one with the help of Dad, me holding the tree in place and them covering up the roots with soil. I water the trees. This is my life now. I want all the flowers Bunica Anghelina had in her garden, so Mom comes home with bulbs and roots—*zambile albastre, lăcrimioare, ghiocei, albăstrele, lalele, crini, bujori, gherghine, trandafiri.** The names of the flowers wash through me again as when Bunica taught them to me and I spend weeks and seasons practicing my "easy hand" with them. I am lucky with flowers; I touch them and they grow, they double. My *bunica* is all over the garden with me now and I feel right and safe. "*Mină caii*, Neculai," I sing to myself and I go over to the cemetery to tell Bunica that I didn't forget the things she taught me. Bunicu Neculai insists on arranging the ceremony for the blessing of the house with the priest who comes bearing basil and holy water as soon as we dig our own family well.

---

* Blue hyacinths, lilies of the valley, snowdrops, violets, tulips, tiger lilies, peonies, dahlias, roses.

Everything seems as new as the morning, smelling of incense while our mouths are filled with sweet drops of communion wine.

Dad arrives home one day smiling and calling Loredana and me from the car. "Kids, come here, I got a surprise for you!" From under his coat peers a little white head with dark eyes, a wet nose, and long white ears. "Meet Bombonica, and don't you dare fight for her!" he says, so excitedly he doesn't realize he is nearly screaming at us.

Loredana and I take the puppy and kiss it and touch its wet black nose. Bombonica, a name invented by Dad, means "little candy," so it sticks perfectly in our minds. Now we have to introduce her to our pitch-black cat.

Hands at the Window

Something is changing at my parents' grocery store. It is a new rhythm that has to do with food and affects how we behave at home. As I am about to turn eleven, I become more interested in listening in to conversations and the news. After all, we are taught in school to educate ourselves by listening to the bulletins transmitted on radio and television. When people talk, they tend to huddle together and whisper.

A truck arrives once a month bringing the rations of sugar, flour, eggs, cold meats, rice, and sunflower oil that the government prescribes for our dietary regime. People save their money for the ration shopping day all throughout the month. Bunica Floarea and Tanti Săftica keep their money wrapped in handkerchiefs closed with tight knots behind the festive plates in their cupboards. If you don't have money on ration day, you starve the whole month. The trouble with the truck is that it never brings all the rations. Getting in line at the stores early is an absolute necessity. The factory cheese workers pack feta or soft cheese in plastic bags and hide them in their rubber boots so that the security guards don't see them. At the slaughterhouses the butchers sneak pieces of meat in their aprons and then hide them inside their clothes. When people are caught stealing at the gates, the guards take half of the food for themselves. So on it goes all the way to the truck drivers who sell lots of the food on the way to the store. The proverb "the early bird gets the worm" proves shaky since getting up and twittering in the food lines turns everyone into early birds. There is always news on television that having too much meat is bad for you and that a proper diet should be made up mostly of pasta and beans. The most important thing the Romanian researchers found out, says the news announcer, is that you should get up from your meal slightly hungry so that you are not sluggish.

Dad and the workers unload the food through the store's back door but my parents are tense because people pester them to sell their rations right away, before the food runs out. They hardly get time to open the front doors. Allegiances are passionately fought: the mayor of the town comes begging for salami; Mom's friends, the town doctor and the pharmacists next door, come asking for their rations of flour or feta cheese. Old women start fighting for sugar because they need it to make jams and fruit preserves. These allegiances must be obeyed, for if the town accountant does not receive his rations, when the time comes for Dad to wait in the really awful line for our monthly cooking gas canister, then we will not get away from the mob with our gas. That daylong line starts the night before in front of the mayor's office. Once every few months, when the store receives its three or four crates of oranges and lemons, the fights are really nasty because each family is allowed only a very few oranges and everyone wants more, especially around holidays when people bake with rinds. Though Mom locks us in her office to spare us the scenes, Loredana and I share her desk chair and perch ourselves to watch everything from the window carved in the door.

The shortages of food are also in the news. The comrades from the Romanian Communist Party carry out searches of those suspected of hoarding sugar and flour in their cupboards, starving the rest of the nation. One evening, the news program has a special feature on catching people "hoarding" food: "Comrades, we are here to investigate the pantry of this family in order to show our great nation why there is no food to satisfy all the rations we are so generously allocated and we work so diligently for in our great factories."

As the reporter speaks, the camera zooms in to the pantry. The family is assembled by the door. The shelves are mostly empty but on one side there is a sack of flour weighing about ten kilos. When questioned about this huge quantity, the family becomes really frightened. Both the husband and the wife are as white as the flour into which the comrade investigator dips his hand. I feel sorry for them as they beg understanding from the camera: "We work long shifts in the factory, comrades. We paid for this flour and we have been keeping it for holiday baking. We paid for it, we worked really hard, we did nothing wrong."

My parents don't know what to do about us children watching the news. Then my father says, "If we want to buy anything to store now, we must bury it in the yard. There are very grim times ahead of us."

Without realizing, I become bilingual as far as feelings go: I learn ease and unease. I am grateful we don't have to grow hungry, thanks to the meat, eggs, cheese, and flour from Bunicu Neculai, and I am afraid that these people who live in towns have nothing in their cupboards except their scrunched-up ration cards. Hungry people are short-tempered, especially men who come from work at the factories, and I can see their faces being sharpened by exhaustion and anger that the rations, even when they are available, do not provide enough food. I start panicking about how Bunicu will keep up the farm and how we will live if he dies.

*

The grocery store is becoming a sort of after-school home where, unintentionally, my parents expose Loredana and me to the realities of life. These have nothing to do with the abundance we hear about at school from our teachers, and for which they say we should be thankful to Comrade Ceauşescu. Dad picks us up and we drive there, sometimes with Bombonica in the backseat. Mom has brought rugs from home to put in her office and we all have plates and cutlery plus a small library of favorite books on the table opposite the desk where she works. We do our homework at the table while she takes care of her paperwork.

Loredana and I know the people who come in for a chat and the people who come in to have wine with Dad at the back of the store, which looks like a small café with one large round table and five or six chairs around it. These are the people with whom Dad listens to Radio Free Europe and the Voice of America and talks politics, something that gets him into huge fights with Mom because listening to these radio stations is illegal and he can be arrested for supporting "anti-Communist propaganda." On the evening programs there are many exiled Romanians who read open letters to Comrade Ceaușescu asking him to release their families to join them in countries they say are "free!" People also read letters about protesters being imprisoned for complaining about shortages of electricity and food in our cities and towns or just for going to church. There is also much discussion about dissidents who are killed and whose families disappear overnight, every week, it seems. In contrast to the Romanian news bulletins during our two-hour television programs in the evenings, where everything in the country seems to be going wonderfully, with factories working full steam, people dancing at cultural shows, and tractors carrying loads of grain to storage houses, the news my dad listens to, of people being killed while attempting to escape at the borders, seems very dark.

From our own radio and television, we only know two things about America: the weekly Sunday episodes of *Dallas,* and people shooting each other on the American streets for drugs or because they are racist. But the Voice of America airs strangely wonderful country, pop, jazz, and folk music programs from places like Nashville and New Orleans and talks about a land where you can become everything you can think of if you work hard enough. The rhythms of country and jazz create images of vast landscapes and never-ending cities in my mind, making me long for some kind of "far away." My dad is receptive to the idea that if you don't like something about the American president, you can just write to him about it. One old woman didn't think Social Security gave her enough money to live on when she retired and after she wrote to the president he announced that he would increase the funds for old people. They also say that if you want to protest, you can make a banner and display it in front of the White House, where the president deals with the business of the country. Sooner or later the TV cameras will come along and you can tell everyone what you are so unhappy about.

"See," says my dad, "this is called democracy. You must be able to express yourself and be respected for your opinions, get a hearing from the people in power. That's what I am talking about. In this place they kill you if you dare complain that the food truck arrived with half the food you were supposed to sell to the hungry folk."

Dad seems to be right. I am glued to the radio, mostly sitting right next to him, and I slowly learn to assimilate two kinds of mutually contradicting impressions about the world in România and the world in the West.

Mom always tries to take me away but I sneak right back to the little "café" as soon as she goes to the front of the store where the real work happens. Other than the rations, there isn't much to shop for save for canned colored peppers stuffed with rice, or tinned pork pâté, or tomato paste and egg pasta. No one buys the other canned food, so every once in a while Mom asks Loredana and me to dust the jars of preserves and the cans of soured cabbage. Kids always come for flavored candy because there isn't much else for them. The conversations between people at the store revolve around the lack of food, weeklong lines at the PECO gasoline stations, and the various kinds of delicacies, such as canned sardines or real coffee, some manage to get at mysterious "black markets." Everyone has to have a "connection" someplace in order to survive, it seems, so listening to Radio Free Europe and the Voice of America becomes a window into a world of truth and plenty.

*

I internalize the rhythm at the store partly by being there and partly by listening to my parents talk about their days. I also learn about my parents' breaking point. When they open for business at around six in the morning, Mom and Dad sell yogurt to people who have been waiting in line since four. Many people bring their summer chaise longues with them to sit while they wait, so the store front generally has a kind of buzz around it. The yogurt comes in small glass jars, tastes sour and soothing, and everyone returns the empty jars to buy the full ones.

At five in the afternoon we prepare for the bread lines. My parents shut all the doors to the store, barricading us inside. The bread truck comes and they unload the loaves through the back; my sister and I often help. We stack all the bread on shelves in front of a small square window on the side of the store. Both Mom and Dad become tense, and so do the store helpers. The smell is incredibly sweet and nutty, rising warmly from the shelves, wafting toward the little square window. Right at five I hear the sound of a coin tapping on the window. Out of nowhere people come, intent to get to the front of the line: small children, barely able to lift their hands to the window, older people with their canes, working people off the bus, children still in their school uniforms. Each one waves the daily ration card and their five lei with a sort of desperation.

There is never, ever enough bread to go around, so people fight each other until the strongest make it to the head of the line. Older people scream and beg Dad to reach toward them with the loaf, women plead with Mom, kids get smashed together, and almost every day some poor old soul passes out. As Mom rushes to call the ambulance, Dad swears violently while my sister and I keep handing out loaves to disheveled people who look like figures painted on the church frescoes of the Last Judgment. All of these hands accumulate in my mind, day after day, week after week, an image of leaves shivering against the glass when I am drifting to sleep. At the end of the bread hour many people go home empty-handed, and I see under the window fallen buttons from overcoats, lost scarves, dropped change, all stamped in the black, dusty earth.

"Let's open the door," Dad says, but instead of going to the front door he walks straight to the back of the store, where he turns on the early-evening news from Radio Free Europe. They say a poet was arrested for writing a poem against the government or someone disappeared for swearing at Comrade Ceauşescu in a bread line. Mom's face looks drawn, dark circles around her eyes. Some days people blame Dad and Mom for the lack of bread and this makes them so angry that Dad begins to talk about leaving the store altogether and taking Mom with him: "We cannot do this day in and day out. Look at you, Mioara, look at us."

There is a thought that occurs to me as a result of helping my parents in the bread lines, and that always bothers me. It has to do with the transformation that people undergo at some point between three and five o'clock. At three everyone is dignified, walking around the small town slowly, calmly, with all the buttons neatly shining on their coats, each face with a pleasant, open smile, which my parents teach my sister and me to imitate, because that is part of being "civilized." At five each person forgets custom and civility and I see neighbors pushing each other, fighting for a loaf of bread. I am not the only one thinking about this; my parents often talk about this change in people's character. Sometimes the Lord's Prayer, which Bunica Anghelina taught me when I was a little girl, comes into my mind: "Give us this day our daily bread." Has this fight for daily bread been the purpose of everyone's existence since God walked upon the earth?

*

There is, I sense, a bit of competition between Mom and Dad about how to raise us. Mom wants us to be educated so that we can have better lives and respect from people. My father wants us to have skills so that we can do things ourselves: build our own fences and shelves, make our own food, repair our own car, install plugs and change lightbulbs and even do some plumbing. Since she was young, Mom has accumulated loads of Russian, French, and English novels from the nineteenth century. She also has books with glossy reproductions of Dutch and Italian Renaissance paintings. With her, life is dreamy, and if she could, she would have my sister and me live in an imaginary place. Many times I look at the eyes that Rembrandt painted until I feel as if they come alive and I am in the painting myself, watching the perfect starched collars and the velvety browns of the sitter.

But when we go around bookshops in Galați on weekend trips, Dad stops at the political philosophy section and reads Marx, Engels, and Lenin, trying to understand where they were so wrong that things are so bad with us. These brief episodes stick in my mind because they provide respite from the general feeling that the purpose of life is to come home with something in the bag to feed the family. It's hard to explain: there are restaurants and grocery stores in Galați and there are cafés, but we only see whitewashed empty walls, peeling wooden shelves.

I read at the house of Aunt Balaşa. Her husband, Uncle Dan, keeps the books behind sliding glass on the shelves; he doesn't like creases in the spines and this is challenging because I cannot lay the books wide open. Also, I love the creases in the book spines because they look like wrinkles on people's faces. Despite these strange habits Uncle Dan has, we spend hours reading and talking about the lives of the characters. The men and women in the novels are concerned with love affairs and with travel; they do not reflect my daily existence, so reading is a kind of escape from one life into another. By contrast, the poems and the stories we read at school all praise our Communist government and Comrade Ceauşescu, who with his wife, the mother of all the children of România, is the father of all of us, something I have known ever since I can remember. Marx, Engels, Lenin, Stalin, and Comrade Ceauşescu share a wall in each of our classrooms and offices. At school we repeat *The Communist Manifesto* mechanically, but it does not represent the kind of struggle I find at my parents' store. Here we are all the same class and we struggle against each other: for basic food. At the age of eleven I can see this but not speak about it, and this is yet another sort of knowledge.

Bunica Anghelina told me when I was in the first grade that when we are taught at school that the existence of God is a "primitive myth" and we must choose "the rational power of man over himself and his own destiny," I must cross myself with my tongue inside of my mouth so that God will see me and forgive me when Judgment Day arrives. "Never, ever lie," my parents tell Loredana and me, but they are so used to lying themselves about things such as God and the Communist Party that they never think to follow their admonition with "except in these circumstances." I confront Mom about this all the time, especially because the more outwardly religious children in my school are taken to the front of the class and punished or insulted by the teachers. When I am made to repeat the phrase "religion is a primitive myth" I automatically cross myself with my tongue in my mouth, asking God to please forgive me. Then I happen to see some of the teachers sneaking into the cathedral in Tecuci or going straight into our village church. I ask myself what the "correct" way is and if "correct" is the same as "right."

One night Dad comes home drunk with a fat goose in his arms. After dinner he goes to bed, bringing the goose with him to watch TV with the family.

"Get the poor thing out of here!" Mom tells him. "Are you mad?"

But Dad, goose hissing in his arms, shouts, "The goose is my work and the TV is my work and I want to sit with both tonight."

The alarmed bird spills droppings all over Mom's beautifully starched sheets. Dad works so little at his repair shop lately, we don't even notice it, until now, when he is proud of having fixed a TV for a goose.

Mom and Dad discuss quitting their jobs at the grocery store. Their conversations are becoming more frequent and heated. The stress of both being treated as saints and being blamed for the diminishing basic supplies drives Dad out of his mind. One day he announces that he would like to try his hand at farming. "So, we'll start with watermelons," he says cheerfully. "We'll rent a few hectares of land on the western side of România from April until August, right at the border, at Oravița where the soil is good. We'll make lots of money selling them in the summer. It's just like taking a few months of vacation! How about that?"

It will take Dad nearly a year to convince Mom.

Burying the Typewriter

Except for the torturous summer mornings when Dad wakes Loredana and me really early to water the whole huge vegetable garden, the grass, and all the flowers, he has the rare talent of turning a boring day into a huge, weird, unexpected celebration. In fact, it is from my parents that I learn to love surprises passionately.

"Children, come," he shouts as soon as he brings our Dacia to a halt. "Your mother and I bought you a typewriter. She is called Erika and she was made in Germany."

His expression is animated, his green-blue eyes glimmering, his arms wrapped around the box. He is definitely more eager than we are to play with this new toy. Wow, but it's not a toy, it's a real one, as big and heavy as an accordion!

Loredana and I peer into the box at the dark yellow-orangey frame, at the black keys, letters and numbers painted in white, grinning like rows of teeth. I didn't think people were allowed to have typewriters in their houses; we only see them in the offices of the school secretary and the police, and where everyone goes to claim the funds for their dead relatives, so they can pay for funerals. My imagination takes off. I am going to *type*. I can see sheets and sheets of paper covered in words neatly arranged like perfect rows of grape bushes in vineyards. I am slightly intimidated, too, for only important announcements or stories or news make it into print, not just anything that might go through my mind. Loredana, the dismantler of everything in the house, jumps from behind me and starts hitting the letters with her forefingers to see how they work while Dad attempts to unclutch her hands from the keys. Mom already worries. "Loredana, please do not take apart the typewriter like you did with the radio and the cars and the doorknobs of the bedroom furniture: promise?"

But who is listening?

*

Soon the village policeman arrives with his helper to complete what I understand to be a "typewriter registration form" with details they receive from my parents: its make, when and where they purchased it, what they are going to type with it, why they need to type food recipes and teach their children how to type. By law, my parents must have the typewriter registered at the store where they bought it. They have to present the paperwork tracing it to the place where they bought it: the police take the "prints" of the machine, its special features that make it traceable—like fingerprinting a person. I admit to unease, thinking about all the detective novels I have been reading recently. Dad says this is just "protocol," we'll all have fun typing things. Mom even has plans to register for an accounting and typing course so she can type without looking at the keys! The uncharacteristic eagerness in my father's explanation of "protocol" leaves a question in my mind. I wonder if my parents have just told us a lie. Typewriters are not exactly something anyone can afford or wants to trouble with, since only writers who appear on Radio Free Europe say they typed poems against the government. Seeing the policeman interrogate my parents and taking so many details about the typewriter makes me feel apprehensive but also vaguely proud. Now we own something only "official" people have. As soon as this is over, Mom lightens up and suggests we find the perfect place for Erika.

*

Our living room has wide windows with white lace curtains through which one can see in at night. The two doors, the double door leading to the veranda and the door leading to the hallway, have big square windows in the top half; matching lace curtains soften the light coming through them. The center of the room is dominated by a heavy oak table covered with a hand-embroidered, perfectly white cloth. At the back of the room, next to the terra-cotta stove running the height of the wall, is a cupboard with a glass and mirror display case in which we store the porcelain tableware, the crystal glasses, and Mom's favorite painted figurines; it makes a sparkling display, even when it is a little dusty. In the afternoons I turn on Radio 3 Iași and listen to classical music or radio drama, all curled up on the sofa, looking at this cupboard. Many times I drift off to sleep to the sound of piano music, and when I wake up the sun has already gone behind the crystal vase to the back of the porcelain dress that Mom's favorite ballerina wears, forever caught in the speed of her pirouette. The light-blue walls are painted with stray silver stars, delicately glowing, shyly, so that as the daylight comes into the blue, they do not outshine each other. At night I can see the wall mirror reflected on the window so the mirror and the chandelier sit comfortably on the grapevine. The room seems to go out at night, and the sky comes in at day. Somehow this room is transparent, magical.

Erika takes up permanent residence on the oak table. At first Loredana and I play with it every day. My sister, perched on the chair, just above the keys, forms with her lips the shape of the letter she is releasing from the row with her right forefinger. As soon as she allows the letter to come out of her mouth, "aaa" and then "sss," there is a sharp, austere slap of metal on the paper, turning the letter into a neat mark. My parents never bother to teach us how to type but keep telling us to "practice" whenever we feel like it. I venture to type my poems until, missing the sound of my pen scratching the paper, my inkwell, and the smell of liquid blue ink, I return to handwriting. Mom takes a typing and accounting course and soon she is fast on the keys, but Dad still types with his two forefingers, which makes him clumsy and frustrated.

*

Loredana and I are no longer visiting the store so often because Dad begins to spend lots of time at home. In the mornings, at around six, the sound of Radio Free Europe comes from my parents' bedroom with news about "repression," "persecution," "cold war." There are increasing pleas from Romanian "refugees" to be reunited overseas with their families. People's open letters to Comrade Ceaușescu are being read on the air. "Do you think anyone in the government listens to this?" I surprise the living daylights out of my parents one morning while I am sipping thoughtfully from my mug of linden tea, holding a piece of bread smothered with jam in the other hand.

Mom jumps. "Carmen," she says, "you shouldn't pay attention to such things. They're not for children. Have you done all of your homework?"

An electrician from Poland, Lech Walesa, speaks against the party there. He is now under house arrest. The secret police take him for random circular drives around the city just to scare him. Dad comments to Mom that simple people can protest too, even if they have to endure interrogations; as long as the international community knows about them they will not be killed. The phrase "political dissident" appears more and more in the news my father listens to.

Dad begins to record the programs. A priest named Calciu-Dumitreasa, now in America, speaks about the horrors he endured in the late 1960s under the Romanian regime. He remembers helping a young man in prison who was also a political dissident. They were both thrown in a basement cell where the water pipes released so much heat it was impossible to breathe. The young man, the priest remembers, fainted on the floor. The priest screamed until the guards came and took the young man outside. My father cries; the whites around his eyes become red, and there are tears running along his cheeks, down his chin. His body is stiff in the chair, poised in the direction of the radio. The young man the priest speaks about is my father. All the time the priest recounts his prison memories, Dad is glued to the radio and me to him. I begin to feel that there is a world of secrets and danger around my parents.

"Dad, tell me about this man, tell me your story, what happened? Mom, will you tell me?" But there is only silence now.

"You are mishearing things and you are imagining stories" becomes the refrain my parents use to greet my questions days and weeks after this incident.

*

Now there are forebodings. Dad is angry that the car keeps running out of gas and he takes turns with his friends waiting in lines, sometimes spending nights sleeping in the car so he can move it closer to the pump while people rush to the early-morning bread or yogurt lines. When Loredana and I go to bed, the typewriter comes to life and makes the only sound in the house. Mom covers the windows in the doors to the living room with heavy towels; she tells us the house is getting colder and we need to preserve the heat. Dad simply locks himself in the living room with a key. The only time Loredana and I get to go into that room now is when my parents forget and leave the door unlocked. The room smells like typescript and carbon paper. The stacks of white paper on the table change size from one day to the next and there are two pairs of thin gloves in the cupboard, where the carbon paper is. Mom complains about wrist pain. In the end, the surprise of the typewriter is not what I imagined when we all stood around it in the summer. Something else is happening to our parents, a change. Though they think Loredana and I don't notice, we feel it in the simplest things such as no longer going to bed at the same time as a family. Then there is the unease of the weekends when Mom and Dad lock themselves in the living room. They ask us to tell visitors that they are not home.

The last of the yellow burns like a struggling torch on the treetops; seasons melt into one another. There are two constant things now: the click of the typewriter and unanswered questions. I am saddened by my exile from the living room.

*

Some days I like to come home from school by way of jumping the fence between the altar side of the church and the back of our house. I appear in the house either with no warning or with a huge thump, depending on how school went. Bombonica always greets me with her wet nose and wiggly tail, probably because she knows that Loredana and I are going to give her fried potatoes as soon as we're out of our school clothes. When I get good grades I love to sling my backpack over the fence and jump as hard as I can. The grass is all gone from the place where I land and there is a path that is almost entirely mine: it goes from the fence into Mom's garden, right under the apple tree.

One day, as I get ready to hop over, I notice Dad standing between the garage and the house. He is digging a big hole just where I am about to jump.

"Hi, Dad, what are you doing there?"

Taken by surprise, he steps aside and turns red from his face all the way down to the top of his chest. "I am making a hole in the ground."

"Why?"

"Hey, leave me alone! Why don't you come home by the road like normal kids do?"

Next to him there is a white plastic barrel cut in two at the fattest part, the middle. Inside the barrel there is Erika, our typewriter, partly wrapped in the green towel that Dad keeps over the living room window.

"What's the typewriter doing here?"

"That's none of your business, Carmenuţo. Chop-chop inside."

"Dad, why is the typewriter here?"

"Because I want to bury it."

I have the sensation of being suspended somewhere between a comedy scene and an out-of-reality zone where weird things happen with no explanation.

"That is *absurd*, Dad. What's wrong with the oak table? I am going to ask Mom why you're burying the typewriter behind the house. It's the strangest thing I have ever seen."

Dad makes a pact with me that if I keep quiet about it he will tell me his reason: "The police keep coming to check the fingerprints from the typewriter and I think I just want to hide it and tell them I sold it back. They are making lots of trouble for a useless thing such as this anyway."

When I go into the living room, Erika sits on the table as shiny as ever. The lie my father just told me weighs heavily on my mind. He and Mom have two typewriters. They type most nights and take these long trips, also at night. They are tense and scared. I am starting to fear that they might be typing anti-Communist flyers of the kind I have been hearing about on Radio Free Europe. I am so scared they are doing this that I do not confront my father about the typewriter but decide to hold on to the secret he told me and keep the one I discovered for myself. Well, okay, I will tell Loredana and will have to swear her to secrecy. We decide to follow Dad around and do some detective work together. Little do I realize, even at this point, what my parents are really up to and what kind of political past my father has, that there is a strong pattern of their doing just this sort of activity. It will be some years before my parents and I will learn that at this point, nearly the end of 1981, there is already an army of Securitate officers who collect these flyers from people's mailboxes and analyze them, hoping to find the two culprits in our living room—to destroy them.

*

There are buckets filled with our freckled beans in the garage—they have been here for weeks and weeks but now I notice them on the other side of the shelf, behind the tools, where Dad spends his days hidden away. Mom and Dad have bought blue overcoats that look like those worn by people selling vegetables at the markets. They take overnight trips "to sell beans" in different towns, they say. I can tell that Dad goes behind the house every night to unearth the typewriter and back there before they leave to bury it: there are regular noises behind the house where I saw him bury Erika. I feel confused and heavy, but no conversation with Dad ever yields anything. The talk all over the village and town is still centered on food, lack of food, the good lines to be in, the bad lines where you wait for nothing. No one thinks anymore; everyone hunts for food. Now electricity is rationed too. After the evening news at seven, the lights go off in every house and on every street. Our village turns into dark shapes with the moon and stars shining on it. People begin to live by the light of candles and flashlights, but these don't last longer than it takes to get ready for bed or have that last glass of wine. My parents light the hurricane lamp Bunicu usually keeps on the side of his cart and continue click-clacking at the typewriter. In the morning, when Loredana and I wake up to get ready for school, the house smells of burned oil.

The Watermelon Child

It's spring 1982. We're at our new home in Drăgănești, us four but not Bunica Floarea, who now comes only in the winter. The trees have not quite grown buds but there are tiny green dots all over them. We're keeping the windows open more often and enjoying the smell of rain as it rushes in. The curtains billow outside the sills when gusts of wind steal them from their sleepy places. Mom is shouting at Dad from the kitchen, where I am reading.

"Nelu, you want to go all the way to Oravița under the pretext of growing watermelons because you want to escape at the border. What do you know about watermelons? You're listening too much to Radio Free Europe. You'll destroy all of us. You know the problems you had before with trying to escape from the country. Have some reason, you have a family life now, we will live like everyone else."

"Mioaro, I just want to grow watermelons. Watermelons! Wouldn't you like to have a whole summer outside? We'll take the children with us, we'll camp the whole time, they will see another side of the country and breathe lots of fresh air. It's what I want. We have time to learn how to grow them, it's just seeds in the ground, and we'll camp by the river and roast corn on the cob. Really. You shouldn't argue with me and worry the children."

When he wants, Dad can be sweet, so sweet you must agree with him, so I tell Loredana all about watermelons. Dad even promises he'll teach us how to drive our car and sell watermelons in the local markets, plus we'll camp in a tent most of the summer.

"That's a whole summer vacation, I mean the whole summer!" shouts Loredana, who is all but ready for packing.

Somehow Dad convinces two families of neighbors and also Tanti Săftica to come along to raise watermelons, so my parents take two weeks off from the store in April for the seeding, and an extended vacation of three months over the summer. The vacation will turn out to be permanent, though, because Dad has no intention of returning to the life at the store, as Mom guessed. This is his way of stringing her along into something she doesn't like. The watermelon experiment is good news to Loredana and me because Mom and Dad have been spending more nights away, are exhausted during the day, clearly doing something we are not supposed to know about but feel is dangerous. Loredana and I intensify our spy missions around the house.

*

We are in the attic playing around the sky window and eating the apples we have kept here since last autumn. Loredana and I wrapped hundreds of bright red and yellow apples in newspapers and stored them in cardboard boxes. We also pickled watermelons, tomatoes, and cucumbers; hung chili peppers and herbs to dry; and stewed eggplant with tomatoes and bell peppers, sealing it in jars for the winter meals. The attic smells of apples all winter long, and since we also store old toys, old books, and unused clothes here, it's a hanging-around place. Mom has kept in labeled boxes all of her teaching notebooks with multicolored diagrams of fruit and various plants explained in botanical terms for her students. (She had to renounce teaching, her favorite job, because she married a man with a political "past." She was taken into the police station and asked to choose, just like that, between her career and her husband. Since she was already pregnant with me, she told the interrogators that she'd like to stay married.) I can feel her nostalgia for teaching when she talks about it. And I love words such as *pistil, deciduous,* and *epidermis* when I read them in her notebooks. I imagine Mom glowing among her pupils as she does when she explains things to us.

What heightens our interest, though, is that Dad now often locks himself in the attic. When I read downstairs I can hear his footsteps shuffling on the ceiling, going to and fro, where there is a table and a crate turned into a chair.

"Hey, there is a big flag here, the Romanian flag," calls Loredana from near the sky window.

"No way! What else did you find?"

Above our heads hangs a huge black cloth banner on which is written in big white letters "I ask for the trial of the Ceaușescu family for crimes against humanity, usury, and the economic downfall of the country!" As I walk backward reading the banner aloud to my sister, I stumble into a big picture frame, which turns out to be the portrait of Comrade Ceaușescu with a black ribbon draped around his face, along the frame, just like portraits of people at funerals.

"Oh my God. He'll definitely get killed if the government finds out and we'll disappear like they say on Radio Free Europe!"

I am shaking, and Loredana is too. There is no way to explain to each other how we feel; it seems like the end of the world. We rush to the living room and take another look at the cupboard where Mom and Dad keep the typing paper. There are stacks and stacks of papers and hundreds of sheets of carbon paper, which we take out and look through to see the marks of the typescript. We read the texts as much as we can but cannot make much sense of what we see. There is, however, in the garage, a stack of typed-up pamphlets, hidden between an old fridge and our bicycles. The text there reads: "We ask for human rights. We ask for freedom of opinion. We ask for hot water and electricity. We ask for freedom to assemble." My suspicions are confirmed. And I feel as if I am losing a sense of what is stable—like the wobbling ground under me in the earthquake.

"This is why they cover the windows in the doors with those towels," I tell Loredana.

"Oh yeah, and the windows facing the street, with the yellow blanket. That's why they don't let us go into the living room anymore!"

"Let's talk to both of them at once," I urge Loredana, while images of Dad and Mom being killed cripple my mind.

A few days earlier we saw the police beat Gypsies at the market in Tecuci because they complained that the bakery didn't sell them bread without ration cards. They argued with the baker, then someone made a call and a gray van suddenly appeared in the market. When the back door to the van opened, men dressed in blue uniforms carrying batons spilled all over the place and started beating the poor Gypsies so violently I nearly vomited and I didn't know whether to run or to stay frozen where I was, holding the hands of Aunt Balașa, whom I was visiting.

Now I can only imagine what will happen to Mom and Dad if they find out about the manifestos. The strange thing is that we had a conversation about the Gypsies at home and it seems Dad wasn't scared. "This is what you call a fight for existence, Carmenuțo," he said. "The Gypsies want food and the police make a living by beating the Gypsies so *they* can get the food themselves. You must have higher ideals in life, you must see beyond your belly. Look what happens in the bread lines every day."

But Mom didn't agree with Dad at all. "Look at you and me, at our work at the store! That is also called a fight for existence. You can't have any big ideals on an empty stomach. You talk like this because you keep the loaf of bread for the town mayor and for the policeman so you don't have to fight with them like the Gypsies. There is nothing I see here other than the fight for existence. Don't look down on anyone."

All I can think of is that I would rather go hungry than get beaten up the way the Gypsies did, and now I must worry about what Loredana and I have found in the attic.

*

"Mom, Dad, we would like to have a family *consiliu* with you now," I announce to my parents over dinner.

We only have family *consiliu* in the most urgent of circumstances, usually when Loredana and I break so many rules that a threat of butt-slapping is simply not enough. Now we ourselves have something to bring to the family conference. I cannot help but feel a bit delighted with myself for raising a serious topic at the table. I feel grown up.

"I found that Dad is preparing stuff for a demonstration against Comrade Ceaușescu," Loredana announces proudly. Her whole body is like a bullet.

"We found a banner and the portrait of Comrade Ceaușescu in the attic," I say solemnly, "and we are scared. On top of that, Dad, I cannot keep your secret anymore. Can you please explain why you bury the typewriter and then you type in the middle of the night? Even better, can you please tell Mom why it was that the day you buried the typewriter in the ground I found the typewriter in the living room at the table? Do you have two?"

Mom goes completely white. She explodes at Dad: "How can you do this while I go to the store and work so hard my bones go through one another? Where are they? This nonsense must be destroyed and this must never happen. I need to talk to you!"

Dad looks first angry, then confused, then disarmed. His face is red but his voice is calm. Clearly Mom doesn't know about the plan for the demonstration.

"My little spies. Look, Miorița, how smart your little girls are. No one can do a thing in this house without them finding out. How about I bring the banners down and we burn everything together in the stove right here in the kitchen and I promise I will never, ever do this again?"

He throws his arms up in a mock desperate gesture: he is actually trying to look *funny*! Why is he giving up so quickly? The three of us wait for him to tell us the truth. We are all quiet. Then he turns serious: "As for the typewriter, yes, we have two, but if you girls ever tell anyone about this, I will be taken to prison and murdered, and you will be taken to an orphanage. This is serious. That typewriter must stay behind the house. I will stop writing everything."

"You promise, right?"

"Yes, but if you tell even one soul about what you saw—and remember you are now ten and eleven, in fact soon coming up to your next birthdays, you are fully grown up—you will basically let the police arrest me and possibly kill me. Do you understand?"

We all solemnly agree to silence, understanding what has happened. We burn everything in the stove, including all the manifestos from the garage, which, to my parents' surprise, Loredana and I bring by armfuls. By the way Mom looks, all scared and stressed, we can tell that while she knew about the flyers, because she helped type and distribute them, she had no idea that dad was planning a protest. Or maybe she is afraid that my sister and I know about what they are doing and we could be telling friends about it, endangering the whole family. In fact there is so much confusion about what they both know and do, we no longer crave clarity. We're learning too much, too fast. More than anything, the two of us yearn for the stability of our parents behaving like everyone else's mom and dad, so we take this chance to clean out every trace of their activities, having earned their promise of a return to "normal life."

*

And so we all go away for the summer in fields filled with watermelons, massive green balls attached to the earth by curly, thin stems. Around our tent there are honeydew melons, smaller and yellow, little suns. The best way to eat watermelons is to snap them off their stems early in the morning before the sun heats them up and cut them exactly in two, scooping up the middle. Each bite releases this incredible cool juice in your mouth and if you feel like breakfast, you can have some bread on the side, like Tanti Săftica.

Loredana and I packed books, clothes, toiletries, beach towels, air mattresses, everything we could get our hands on for the long time away from home. We bathe in the river next to the watermelon farm, our neighbors' children too. Tanti Săftica is all tanned, and I am learning how to drive with Loredana and Dad, every once in a while crushing watermelons when we practice the reverse gear. As Dad promised, we roast corn in the evenings and sing songs. Sometimes we go to nearby villages to get things from the bakeries and we buy whole chickens from the peasants to grill. The river is deep, sheltered by ancient willows whose branches we swing from as we throw ourselves into the water, once again playing at being Tarzan in the jungle. The bottom of the river is soft and claylike, muddy; when we pop up, the water turns a kind of yellow.

Mom has a belly. There is a belly inside Mom's shirt. Mom is not feeling so well and her belly is growing bigger. This is the summer when I am growing breasts and I haven't a clue how they got there or what I am to do with them. Everything is weird. Tanti Săftica, because Mom is so shy, tells Loredana and me over lunch at her tent that Mom is expecting a child in February, so we should be thinking about taking care of a new brother or sister. Months later when I touch Mom's belly I feel the child kick. Loredana and I are envious and angry: everything has been split in two, for me and for her. Now everything must change.

"It's the watermelon vacation your Mom and Dad needed," Tanti Săftica tells us, "and sometimes watermelons just lead to people being happy and making babies. I feel you will have a baby brother."

As Mom's belly swells, toward the autumn, we spend the time hardly selling anything but playing and eating watermelons. Loredana and I invent my brother's name: Bostănarul, "watermelon boy." Or maybe we hear Mom and Dad call him this and we think we invented it. Mom keeps talking about a dream she had one day, at the beginning of her pregnancy. She was about to have an abortion so she made an appointment with the gynecologist. The day of the appointment she took a nap and dreamed that Saint Mary came out of a pink and purple sky with an angel and a boy, holding them by the hands. She told Mom she'll have a wonderful boy. Mom never went to the doctor, so the child from the dream grows in her belly.

*

Nearly every day a man comes on a motorcycle to "visit" Dad. They go a little way from the tent, at the edge of the field. There is an air of secrecy around them, but from what we can glean, Loredana and I think he is from the Securitate and is interested in why Dad chose to spend the whole summer so near the border. We also find out, through overhearing broken conversations between Mom and Dad, that Dad spent seven years in prison before we were born, before he met Mom, because he protested against the Communist regime and tried to escape from the country. The story of the priest saving the young man in prison comes back to me and I know there are more secrets about my father. Loredana and I are so uneasy about this new information and about the man who comes to speak with my dad that we only want to think about our watermelon brother. But before we get a chance to sell off the watermelons, we are sent back home by the police, who tell Dad he is "unfit" to spend any more time this close to the border. Once we are there, both parents without jobs, lots of money wasted during the summer and the watermelons abandoned to rot in the fields, the *click-clack* of the typewriter returns furiously and in the garage I find big sheets of black cotton, paintbrushes of different sizes, white paint, nails. Of course, my father never had any intention of ending his activities when he burned everything in the stove. Neither had Mom.

Worse still, Loredana leaves for gymnastics school at Oneşti. I stay home with Mom and Dad, sharing the candlelight, the flashlight, their secrets about which we no longer speak. My time is spent deeply lost in reading Romanian novels about summer vacations and first loves. I start thinking about what it might feel like if I kissed a boy. I am trying to escape the tension in the house. This summer I turned twelve.

*

Winter arrives but this year Bunica Floarea does not come to the house. I suspect this has to do with Mom and Dad doing their strange typing and traveling. After Christmas Mom begins to feel ill from the pregnancy, so she goes into the hospital for about a month. I go to see her once a week and spend the rest of the time with Dad, who does his best to send me to Tanti Săftica for after-school snacks or for dinners. I also visit Bunicu Neculai, who is beginning to forget things, including my name sometimes. Because I am now old, I must do the rounds in the bread lines. I am no longer the child handing out loaves from my parents' store. Now I am one of the people being smashed and cursed on the way to the baker's hands and I am also shy. I cannot bring myself to fight with old people or with children, so everyone gets ahead of me. Most of the time I come home bruised and empty-handed unless the baker notices me. Dad tries to help too: he takes the bicycle and heads to Tecuci with our unused ration cards but he might spend half a day just to come home with one loaf of bread or frozen vegetables. Because we know that informers stand in lines in order to report on anyone who complains, we both agree to make no comments when we are out shopping. We eat so much polenta and fried canned cabbage and boiled beans, my stomach hurts like hell. I miss Mom and Loredana. I am lonely, so I read. We still get the milk from Bunicu, so at least that is taken care of.

On February 2 my mother sends word from the hospital that she had a baby boy. Dad and I buy silk flowers and rush to the maternity ward. She appears at the window, pale and beautiful, holding a white bundle in which she cradles a bluish face. When we bring her home, she shows us my brother's bandages all around his neck and shoulders. It was a complicated birth, so his shoulder bones had to be broken for him to come out. He is ill, he is small. I look at him with detachment and fear, and yet with a kind of affection, which is mostly pity. He is so weak he can barely cry, he is so very small; I want to keep him in my arms until I go numb. As days go by and he continues to breathe, I come to fear for him less and I beg Mom to name him Cătălin, a name from Eminescu's poem *Luceafărul* about the distant star that fell in love with a beautiful mortal girl named Cătălina. I decide that my brother should be earthly, beautiful, and innocent as the blond, rosy-cheeked Cătălina, because the life of the genius, the outcast thinker is a lonely one. I want him to love the earth and the forests and the food so he can live without suffering. For myself, I want to be like the cold star in *Luceafărul* and hold in me everyone else's pain, though I am not sure I can do this outside the boundaries of the poem. It is I, more than anyone else, who love the earthly life. So Mom and Dad and Loredana, who comes home briefly to see our new brother, agree: he is to be named Cătălin. When he becomes ill a few weeks later and goes into the hospital with Mom, I am back alone with my father in the empty house, worried and depressed.

March 10, 1983

At around two in the morning, my father finally turns the radio off. The Voice of America goes quiet and I can hear Bunica Floarea's snoring. It's good to have her back, even if Dad says it's only for a few days. I have turned into Dad just by spending so much time with him. We hardly ever disturb each other with questions and we have been spending dinners in silence eating whatever cooked food I manage either to bring from Tanti Săftica or to prepare really quickly, usually polenta with fried eggs. We listen intently to Radio Free Europe and the Voice of America, he spends the days in the attic or garage, and after school I study undisturbed.

By now studying is a release, so I pile the books and notebooks by subjects on the big table in the kitchen and lose myself in ancient history, geography, literature, math, physics, French.

"Carmen, come and close the gates. No, just the front door. Tell them nothing."

I get up and walk after him. "There is nothing but a bit of fried cabbage left to eat. When are you coming back?"

"Well, Carmen, *ai să mănînci tată și foc*—you'll even eat fire. I must go now."

Earlier in the day we had fought. It was a hard fight. I saw Dad preparing the car for his trip. On top of the car was the bike rack, but on it there were mounted two placards, covered with gray cloth. Inside the car were sacks with leaflets, topped off with the same dry beans I have seen around the garage for months and months.

"I will take nails and hammer them into the car tires so you cannot go anywhere."

It wasn't difficult to imagine what he would do, and I was frightened for my life. The stories I heard on the radio stations Dad listened to were stories about people who were tortured or vanished. Entire families disappeared because one of the parents said or did something against the regime. I have not a soul to speak with or consult about trying to contain him. Mom is still in the hospital with Cătălin and Loredana away at her gymnastics school.

"What will you do in Bucureşti?"

"I am just going to bring someone from the morgue, that's all. Leave me!" he yelled at me. His eyes were bloodshot, his two-day-unshaven face looked pale, he was an intense pile of nerves. I was too afraid to destroy the tires of the car.

Now I turn the lock in the door and the sound of gates closing is followed by the sound of the engine breaking the sleep of the street. Then it is silence. Bunica Floarea is still asleep, innocent as an old angel.

*

In the morning I go to school hoping that he is not discovered, that he really is bringing someone he might have known back from the morgue, and that he will just drop some leaflets and change his mind about the placards. I think he is naive. In America things happen differently with protests, but in România we no longer need Radio Free Europe to see government repression. One person in three is an informer for the Securitate and everything happens through bribing the Securitate, because, in the end, they want to make money and secure food for themselves as well. They are people just like us. We are all learning to accept the simple fact that someone is pulled from the bread line and taken away for comments like "Goddamn, where is my loaf of bread?" I cannot concentrate on my classes and I cannot focus on the usual chatter with friends. I am relieved to hear the bell.

*

Bombonica barks as if someone is tearing her apart. I am changing clothes in my bedroom so Bunica Floarea goes to the gate, shuffling in her blue plastic slippers. By the time I make it to the veranda, wrapped in Mom's gray cardigan, a car is parked outside the gates and there are men wearing suits already walking toward me, with the dog continuing to bark at them as if she is seeing the mouth of hell. Maybe dogs have intuition.

"I am the chief of the Securitate in Tecuci and these are officers from the district office. You must be Carmen. We would like you to sit down and answer some questions now." They settle comfortably in the armchairs without Bunica or me inviting them. I do not like that at all.

"I have school tomorrow and will need to get to homework soon, so I hope to answer your questions as quickly as possible."

"Where is your father?"

"Gone to bring a dead person from the morgue in București."

"Who is the dead person?"

"I don't know."

"Did you see the car when he left?"

"No, he left early in the morning and I only got up to lock the door. I was sleepy."

"Did he go alone?"

"Yes."

It is now one in the morning and their questions, repeated over and over again, in different words, jumble in my mind. My mouth is dry, I struggle to swallow. They ask who types at the typewriter, and I say that all of us type recipes and sometimes I type my poems or poems for friends. No one knows about the other typewriter but this one is confiscated along with all the food from the house: the bottle of sunflower oil, bread flour, olives, rice, polenta, pickled vegetables, fruit jams, the leftover apples we kept over the winter—everything. The officers tell me that this food will be transferred to the village shop to be sold and that we shouldn't have so much flour in the house. I tell them that the flour for bread and polenta is from Bunicu Neculai, who has taken his own grains and corn to the village mill since I can remember. I notice, but do not argue with the officers, that the food is split in smaller portions and taken to the car to be distributed among them. The sight of olives, apples, and jams awakens in their faces expressions that resemble pleasure: they will take our food for their families. This is confirmed weeks later, when Bunicu asks the shopkeeper about selling our food and the shopkeeper is oblivious. Bunica Floarea is interrogated in the living room separately; I hear only the jumble of words, muted by the closed doors. I am annoyed that none of these people are taking their shoes off, and Mom will be angry with me when she finds our perfectly clean rugs bearing the marks of so many dirty shoes.

"Do you receive foreigners at the house? Does your father have friends from overseas?"

"No. How would they get here?"

"Are there any weapons in the house?"

"Since you are searching the whole house and confiscating the food, why don't you see for yourselves? I have never seen any."

"How old are you?"

"Twelve."

"Do your parents listen to Radio Free Europe and the Voice of America?"

"What are those?"

"Do your parents participate in anti-Communist propaganda?"

"No. Why would they?"

"Why did your father record this priest speaking about his prison time in the 1960s?"

"I don't know why or who he is. I go to school every day and then I do homework and play with friends."

"Do you know why your father has all these rolls of ribbon with our national flag colors?"

"No. Where did you find them?"

The family portraits come off the walls one by one and are stripped until the backs of the photos are revealed, bruised by the knives with which they cut the protective layer of paper. The tapestries my parents pinned to the walls come off, lutes, mandolins, and Turkish dancers now crumpled on the floor. All the bedding in the house is taken off and shaken, the sheets, then clothing, tablecloths are all pulled out from the closets and piled on the floor. The cutlery, plates, china, crystal, the papers are all brought down from the cupboards around the house and piled on the floor. The rugs are turned upside down. The library is dismantled and the spaces behind the books are opened and searched, furniture pushed to the middle of each room. Our rooms are sealed with red wax that is heated, pressed, and stamped on top of knots made of rope, over the door handles: the house is becoming "an investigation scene." Everything is torn with a brutality which simply discounts the fact that a family lives in and loves this house. It is as if we do not exist anymore. Bunica and I are given limited access to the kitchen and the bathroom. From this night on we are not allowed to go through the rest of the house, even to get a change of clothing. I am taken to the doors, shown the seals, and threatened with "criminal intent" if I go into any rooms. Before we are sent to bed, Bunicu Neculai, whom I didn't notice arriving, is sent home with the threat that if he comes to feed us or to talk to us, he will end up in a ditch or in jail. I hear the conversation, I hear Bunicu saying, "But the poor girl, let me at least take her home with me. She is just a child," and I feel like crying and running to tell him not to worry, I will be okay.

I finally curl up with Bunica on one of the two beds we keep in the kitchen, both with our day clothes on. The Securitate does not leave. The men settle into the living room, smoking the cigarettes they "confiscated" from my parents. They make plans for digging in the yard in the morning. It hasn't been long since yesterday, yet everything I have known has collapsed around me.

*

At six the next morning the village policeman, whom I know, wakes me up, saying: "Carmen, we must ask you some more questions."

I am told that today I will be allowed to go to school when classes start. What I am not told, however, is that for the next few weeks my schoolgoing schedule will be interrupted by frequent interrogations and that when I show up at school after long absences I will be reproached for being a bad, lazy student. I am asked the same questions, with new wording, again and again. I am told I am not to speak with any of my friends at school about anything.

"When will my father come home?"

"You may not see him for a very long time, or you may never see him. But a lot depends on how much you can help us with your answers."

When I return from school, where everyone already knows about the "search" at our house, the garage looks like a huge spiderweb, antennae and wires all over the place. I am not allowed to go in there. Men holding metal detectors signal to men digging by the well, where they uncover a few bottles of sunflower oil. Dad and Mom bought this oil a long time ago, when we heard that the rations would get tougher. There are seven or eight bottles and we forgot all about them, it's been so long. I see the Securitate men take the bottles and divide this coveted food among themselves, placing them in the backseat of their car, "confiscating them." Sunflower oil is a delicacy these days: people use it only on salads; cooking is done with lard. When we use oil for frying, Dad always tells me to keep it in the pan and fry things in it day after day, until the oil gets dark, and never to throw away any drops of it unless it is clearly burned. This "confiscation" makes me angry. I am not allowed to go out to buy food, and Bunica and I are not given anything to eat. The man who divides the bottles equally has round cheeks and almond-shaped eyes. Small, with small fat hands, he doesn't show the slightest expression of guilt; it seems he has been rummaging through people's houses for food forever. When he returns to the well, the turned-up earth sits like a black bruise at his feet.

*

For the past three weeks I have been living on water and walnuts Bunica found in a corner of the kitchen, where they were overlooked

by the Securitate. Much of this time I have not been allowed to go
to school. I have had to answer the same questions again and again.
Bunica discovered some *florio*, Mom's homemade sherry, and she drinks
mouthfuls of it once a day then paces the yard talking to herself. It's
not hard not to eat. There are new interrogators coming every day and
I watch how they set microphones around the house, testing them in
the garage. They now have keys, too, and they come back and forth
day and night, so often that to go to the bathroom I have to wake up
Bunica and ask her to wait at the door.

Still there are questions and I am tired of saying that I don't know
any people from other countries, that I don't think Mom and Dad
typed any anti-Communist propaganda at the typewriter, and that
I never was aware of anything my parents have said or done against
Comrade Ceauşescu. I am truly determined to tell them nothing,
just as my father told me the night he left. So is Bunica, who is not
intimidated by them, but is tired of asking where my parents and my
sister are and when any of them will please be coming back home.
We are both weak. We are sleeping with our day clothes on until
they smell like vinegar. I have many hallucinations about angels and
Bunica Anghelina and Mom and Dad and big meals.

One morning, the village policeman taps me on the shoulder,
puts his finger over his mouth, motioning to keep quiet, and gives
me bread from a loaf. He hands Bunica some too. After we built the
house he used to come around asking Dad to fix his car, as Dad used
to fix everyone's cars, either because they were friends or because
people gave him chickens, eggs, homemade butter, stuff like that. His
full moon-shaped face looks pale and nervous; as he watches me eat,
his complexion takes on a shade of gray from his uniform. But he is
in an official position now, so he acts as if he doesn't know my family well. There is nothing else we can tell at the daily interrogations,
regardless of how weak we are. I haven't taken a bath in three weeks
and I beg for some privacy to wash myself.

*

One day, another black car parks outside the gates, again filled with men in suits and leather coats.

"I am Colonel Coman. I am here so you can tell me about the buried typewriter." Colonel Coman appears to me a friendly, smart man. I can look into his eyes without looking upward too much.

"What do you mean, the 'buried' typewriter?"

"Your father gave me directions to the back of the house, between the garage and the kitchen walls, on the path."

"I am sorry but I don't know about this. Where is my father? How is he? When is he coming home? No one has told me anything about him for weeks now."

"I am very sorry but this is not the time to speak about your father. Can you tell me who typed at this second typewriter?"

"But I only ever saw Erika and we all typed recipes and poems and silly things. I don't know what my father told you."

"Okay, how about we go to the back of the house and my helpers here will dig for it?"

I follow them to the garden like a paralyzed person thinking to myself, no, no, don't find it please. They look at a map drawn by my father during his interrogation and begin digging. Wrapped in the green towel that Dad usually kept over the window in the living room door, the typewriter comes out of its white plastic barrel hidden in the hole. Yes, this is the illegally owned typewriter my parents bought in Bucureşti, from a secondhand shop, taking advantage of the salesgirl's absentmindedness, as she forgot to ask them for their identity cards. It is the typewriter Dad buried and dug up day after day, the one he said he would never use. I feel my cheeks burning red and I hope they do not see or understand that I have been lying to them. This typewriter goes with the colonel in his car. At least I am left with the knowledge that Dad is still alive, though I haven't a clue what will happen next.

*

"Carmen, Carmen, oh God, the things that happened to me. What did Dad do? I was doing exercises in the gymnastics room when these men came and asked me about Mom and Dad typing manifestos. I said I didn't know anything."

I cover Loredana's mouth and take her outside. "Shhh, there are microphones everywhere." I am so happy to see her!

"Dad left me alone here with Bunica Floarea in the middle of the night and went to Bucureşti with manifestos and placards. The whole house is sealed. I tried to get hold of Mom in the hospital to tell her what happened, but the Securitate says I am not permitted to call her or write to her or to go to Galaţi to see her in the hospital. They starved Bunica and me for three weeks. We have no father anymore. He left us. I fought with him, but he left us anyway."

I am trying to make sure Loredana understands our new situation, so I grab her hands. She pulls away and talks very fast. "They said I couldn't leave the dorm at all and every time I tried to go to the shop next to the school someone took pictures of me on the street and my teachers got in trouble when I left the school grounds. I found glass in the cafeteria food all the time so I got really scared of eating. My God, what will happen to us? I am so scared! They said I am thrown out of school now so I should come home."

Loredana is intimidated. Her nervy body is now nearly nervy bones, her chest bones visibly panting through the turtleneck sweater. Yet as we take each other's hands I sense so much strength in her grip, I feel grounded by her presence. Choppy hair sitting thick on her forehead over her dark eyes, cheeks red with emotion, lips red with emotion, she is like fire. She has always been the stronger of us. Whenever I did something wrong I asked her to tell Mom and Dad that she was the guilty one because I was too afraid or ashamed of the punishment. She took the punishment nearly all the time, not letting their words affect her the way they stung me. Now she is home and I am reassured with her at my side. Bunica Floarea rushes to warn us not to speak in the house. It is the first month without our parents. Life is suspended. Questions hover over painful silence.

*

It's mid-May. Next month I will be thirteen years old. The torn yard is covered with healing grass, flowers crowd around the doorstep. Loredana and I are now both going to the village school followed every day by the same man from the Securitate. We baptized him "the Chinese" because he is short and has long, almond-shaped eyes. We already know he has taken a room in the house of the village veterinarian at the corner of our street, from where he watches everyone who comes to and goes from our house. Even though we are told we are not permitted to go anywhere but to the village shop to buy our rations of food and to school, we walk regularly to see Tanti Săftica and Bunicu Neculai because there is nothing the Securitate men actually do to stop us. Family friends drop cooked food in little jars at Tanti Săftica's and together with what she can give us, we receive enough for ourselves and Bunica Floarea to survive. My sister and I wait for the jars with chicken soup, vegetable stews, rice, beans in tomato sauce, and we are grateful.

School is different. No matter how hard we study and how well we prepare for the daily lessons, Loredana and I are earning low grades and lots of abuse from the teachers, right in front of the other students. The Securitate tells us at home that we are poor students, that we make bad pioneers, and that the teachers are complaining about our performance. It is worrying. My history teacher asks me to stand up in the middle of the class, declaring, "Your father is a mentally ill criminal who is destroying your future." The other children are encouraged to taunt us and on the playground they throw stones at me, calling me "daughter of criminal." No one comes to my defense. Because the Chinese walks behind us on our way to school and after school, kids have picked up on this as well, laughing at us because we can no longer play freely after classes, like they do. Loredana and I are trapped, and our isolation is made more painful when they laugh at us because our father refused to compromise and live a life of silence in the face of oppression.

*

"Carmen Bugan, go immediately to the teachers' office!" announces the literature teacher gravely. She just burst in during the math class. My stomach turns into a knot so fast it hurts. She is stiff and quiet until the door to the office closes and only the two of us are inside. Then she takes from her handbag a huge slice of bread, a few thick slices of salami and cheese. "Eat, do not speak a word now or to anyone," she says. She has tears in her eyes as she goes to listen at the door for anyone coming down the hall. I obey and I eat. Tears and food taste so good together. Then she brushes the crumbs from my uniform, wipes my eyes, and takes me back to the math class.

This ritual, under the pretext of some kind of punishment, now happens a few days every week. I can show no gratitude except by eating her food. With time, she will become the reason I believe that literature truly nourishes the hungry. She will become the reason I love morphology and syntax, and she will suffer with me through my family's nightmares and through my intense love of poetry, which often makes me confuse the worlds of imagination and reality. I will never, for the rest of my life, know or love a teacher more. Her name is Lucia and her own story will emerge slowly to me over the years, but now she is the literature teacher with the sandwiches.

*

At the end of May, Mom appears in the house. There is no warning. Bombonica doesn't even bark. Bunica and Loredana are around somewhere—at the well or feeding the chickens—and as I fumble by the stove, Mom opens the door with Cătălin in her arms. She sobs so much and I sob so much that we don't manage any words between us for a while. And then her face toughens. "Carmen, you are no longer a child. From this moment on, you are an adult who needs to behave like a grown-up woman who handles serious responsibilities. Do you understand? From now on, you are no longer a child."

I want to cover her mouth and tell her there are microphones in the house but instead I say I understand this very well and I am already grown up now. I take Cătălin from her arms. He is just waking up from his child dreams, smiling so beautifully that I cry again. I set him down on the bed and then write to Mom on a page at the back of my notebook: "There are microphones all over the house, recording us. I didn't tell anything about manifestos or knowing about Dad, or about the second typewriter. Loredana did not say anything either. We're okay here. Please don't talk about this or let's talk outside, in the garden."

"So, where is Loredana and where is Bunica?" she asks aloud, as if I haven't scribbled anything. I set the paper on fire in the stove.

"They should be around."

"What have you been eating? You look awfully thin. I need to find a job now, that's the most important thing."

"How is Cătălin's health? Do you have a diagnosis?"

We are exchanging meaningful information but we are also following a script, for no word about Dad enters the conversation. We choose what is safe to say to the microphones, for in this reality we are speaking *for* them.

"The doctors say he has a condition called *malabsorbție* and there isn't really a cure for it. We need further testing. He eliminates protein. He needs a special diet of liver, carrots, rice, and vitamins."

"I can go around and ask the neighbors to give us the liver from all the chickens, when they cut them. How about I go now?"

As I stumble out of the door on my first errand as a grown-up woman, determined to beg for every carrot and liver in the village, I see the Securitate visitors arriving to interrogate Mom at home. I get out of the way and let the man I know all too well, as my own interrogator, meet Mom. But I am an adult and there is no way this little man will mess with my will to win life back. I go find Loredana to tell her about my errand. It's good to see that, after all, my mother, my sister, my brother, and Bunica Floarea are back under the same roof, right here in our house, even if the doors are locked and sealed with red wax. Not only this, but Loredana, animated by having something important to do, is coming with me to beg for livers and carrots.

*

Securitate or not, people begin coming to give us little pale chicken livers "and the heart, for the boy, so he grows hearty and strong." We boil them straightaway, mix them with vegetables and rice, and feed Cătălin. Bunica is washing the cloth diapers while my brother giggles at Bombonica. Mom is allowed to work in Tecuci at the factory that weaves wicker baskets. It's a grim place, a huge unheated room made entirely of cement, smelling of water and soft willow branches. You have to keep the branches soaking in cold water and work with them while they are wet. When you twist and bend them you need to use a strong grip or else they come out loose as you try to tie them. Mom's hands and wrists hurt from twisting and tangling; she has to make a certain number of baskets every day or else she is harassed by the managers. Her fingers swell up and her hands get stuck when she opens and closes them.

The Securitate confiscated her Communist Party card, arguing that she is "unfit" to teach school or to work in the grocery store because her marriage to a political agitator means she is likely to "pollute the minds of the people." Before she was finally allowed to work weaving baskets she begged our village mayor to give her a job milking cows at the cooperative farm, so she could at least be closer to home, but she was refused even this job because she was "unfit." We don't know if the whole village is afraid of Mom now because the Securitate is after her day and night or if the lady mayor wants desperately to show how much of a "clean" Communist she is herself. When my parents fought over Dad listening to the dangerous radio stations, he called Mom a "card carrier"; now the party has its turn at hurting her feelings.

But we no longer mind so much being classified as "unfit members of society" and "social garbage" because we are concerned with survival.

We have a simple schedule: everyone is to stick to the routines, the family is to travel always together for shopping at the weekend, and we are to know each other's individual work and school schedules. If anyone is ten minutes late coming home, we will assume something awful has happened: a car accident, Securitate interrogation, something dangerous. We function together like the hands on a clock: Mom works days in the factory and at night knits sweaters to exchange with her friends for food, Loredana and I go to school and raise Cătălin, while Bunica keeps an eye on the house and helps us. We are learning to look behind our backs and recognize the shadows as Securitate men, not trees in the dim lights of the road. We learn to *always look* behind our backs and be aware of being followed so we can stick to public, well-populated places.

Since my father left on March 10, we have had no news from him, and months later, we are losing heart as people around the village tell us they heard he is dead. Then one night Mom has a dream.

Mom's Dream

The grass in the churchyard grows juicy, thick blades, perfect for feeding our chickens. Bunica has arranged with the priest to let us cut bagfuls in the mornings and evenings, so Loredana and I jump over the fence behind the house with small hand scythes. Sometime we take Cătălin along and set him on a small blanket where he giggles away at the saints painted on the outside walls. The priest is friendly; if he happens to be around the church he comes for a chat. We tell him about the Securitate, mostly because we trust him enough to admit to him that we are afraid and that all the rumors about Dad having killed himself or having been killed are taking their toll on the family.

"Mom cried last night," Loredana tells him one day. "She said she would be grateful to see Dad even as a very old man, after years and years of prison. Even though their life together was being cut short by Dad's absence, she would still be happy, she said, as long as she could see him."

And I say that we cannot talk openly in the house because of all the microphones registering everything. "The other day, the veterinarian told Mom that the guard staying at her house, the one who looks Chinese, bragged about how he can hear even the little sobs of my brother through the microphones. But we have nothing to hide, you see, and everyone in the village knows about our situation, anyway. The Securitate don't let us draw the curtains at night because they want to see inside."

The priest points to a large metal box on a thick branch of the poplar. "That's a strange-looking box. Do you know when it was placed there?"

"Yes, I saw them set it up, but you know, Father, the Chinese informer tests the microphones in the cornfield that belongs to the blind old woman next door, so they put stuff everywhere."

Because I know too well that some of the priests also work for the government, I am instantly sorry for trusting this man so much, for bursting out like that. I guess I couldn't help the old instinct that you "confess" to the priest and then it's his own trouble with God if he takes in vain or wrongly what it is that weighs in your heart—I learned that from Bunicu when I was little. Every Easter Loredana and I had to go to confession at the church with the rest of the children in the village. We all crowded under the priest's vestments and he asked, "Have you lied? Have you stolen? Have you taken God's name in vain? Have you spat on each other? Did you beat and curse each other? Have you disobeyed your parents?" To all these questions we had to say yes whether we committed all these sins or not, that's what Bunicu told us. Then the priest would tell us all to go and kneel ten times, say ten Our Fathers, and come back on Easter Day for Communion. Magically, at Eastertime there were no teachers waiting for us at the church gates to write our names in the ledgers and punish us all at school for our religious practices. In fact, I know that our teachers themselves went to confession!

A few days later, in the afternoon, the priest comes to the churchyard with a few men, swinging his robes, pleased with himself. From the kitchen window, I see axes and a tree-cutting saw. All I can think of is the box: "Oh my God, he'll knock over the box and he'll get arrested." I grab Bunica and Loredana—we all go to the window, eyes bulging as big as onions. One by one, the lower tree branches come down and then the men begin sawing in earnest at the trunk of the poplar. As the tree goes crashing alongside the painted wall where Mary and Joseph walk with their donkey and cane, the cables from the box pull the antennae from the top of our garage, sending the whole listening arrangement crashing. The priest orders the men to chop the trunk carefully for winter wood, and, acting as if he doesn't know what the box is for, yanks the cables from inside, trying to dismantle the contraption. I want to rush over to kiss him but I am also afraid for him.

"Ahah, hah, hah," Bunica laughs. "Now let's see the little shitters fight with the man of God."

No sooner has she finished the sentence than the policeman comes running from the entrance of the church in alarm. As he gesticulates to the priest and his men, asking about the tree, the Chinese man rushes over as well, and two other Securitate informers soon appear. It has taken only about ten minutes for these people to show up, so now we are in no doubt that we're directly under their eyes. Fragments of the conversation come through the window.

"Oh, this tree is so rotten and old I thought we'd better cut it up for winter wood in the church. . . . Oh, the box? What box? What is that for? How is it that you didn't come to inform me about this box, son? This is church property. What is it used for, anyway? Why is it connected to the Bugans' garage? Sorry, my dear son, what do you say? God bless you. Go in peace."

*

I am sitting on the floor at Mariana's house, where Mom goes to talk in peace. Mom and Mariana's husband, Marcel, were childhood friends. For many years the two women have had a strong bond; both are interested in gymnastics for their girls, Loredana and Gina, and love reading, while the men like to fix cars together. I used to go to their house with Loredana when we lived with Bunica Anghelina because Marcel's mother used to give us lots of her apricot jam on homemade bread. We would eat so much jam that she could stop us attacking the jars with big spoons only by saying that too much of it would make our belly buttons tie up in big knots. Mom's visits now are almost all about speaking openly, out of the microphones' hearing.

"How did you survive being away from the children for two months?" Mariana asks, handing Mom a small cup of tar-black coffee, which looks more bitter than it tastes.

"They came in the afternoon the day Nelu demonstrated in București and interrogated me for two months, giving me enough privacy only to breast-feed Cătălin. Day and night. Many times I fell asleep in the armchair answering questions, with Cătălin in my arms, almost always the same questions. They wanted to know every detail of our lives since the moment we met. And I had to write most of it down; they compared one written report to another to see if there were any discrepancies. The doctors and nurses were anxious because they had never seen so many Securitate officers in the hospital."

Mom drinks a sip of coffee and continues. "It was unbearable to go day by day without being allowed to call home. I didn't know what had happened with the girls. By the end I went mad and they said I was having 'psychiatric episodes,' but in truth I was screaming and talking with Cătălin. Some days I went to the hospital gates and kneeled with Cătălin in my arms, praying aloud that I would see my family again."

Mariana's eyes are becoming slightly red, but Mom doesn't notice, lost in her own emotions.

"You know, I love Nelu but there are moments when I feel it will be hard to forgive him for doing this to us, for being more concerned with politics than with his own children. I mean, trying to change the country, yes, but if it is at the expense of your own three children, then where's your perspective, your compassion? At one point Carmen was in town, I knew, for a district math competition but she wasn't allowed to see me. I begged and begged and finally they sent me home. Cătălin is not well and it's impossible to get a referral to a specialist."

Mom is now thirty-seven years old. She nearly fits into my clothes, she is so small and thin, and when she gets angry she is just like Loredana, a released bullet. I feel betrayed by Dad too, and I have to think hard about it. He behaved selfishly toward us, it's true, even if he is right about the need for a revolution. I don't often hear Mom talk like this. But when she does, the strength coming from her body, her breath, her eyes is so powerful that I cannot imagine her being brought to her knees.

*

I wake up to the sound of Mom speaking softly with Bunica Floarea.

"Mother, I dreamed I was walking up a stone road to a gated building. There was a young soldier at the entrance. He led me up some steps. To the right of the main door I saw our car parked in a covered space. And then the soldier led me to Nelu. He is alive, I am certain of it."

I go to them and ask, "How did Dad look? Was he okay?"

Bunica sighs and says, "I hope your dream is true. Jana came by earlier to tell me there are rumors that he killed himself."

*

There is blood, I am bleeding. I don't know what to do so I cry in the bathroom loud enough that Mom can hear and ask me what is wrong. I show her the stained toilet paper, feeling as if the world has opened a great huge hole beneath my feet. I am anxious, I fear I am very ill. Mom doesn't say anything but starts weeping while she holds me.

"Am I going to die, you think? Why is there blood here?"

She grabs a piece of cotton from the pharmacy bag where we keep supplies for cleaning up bruises and cuts, makes a sanitary pad of it, and gives it to me, showing me how to use it. "It will stop in about three days. Oh God, Carmen, you are a woman now." And she runs outside.

I am shaking. A few minutes later Bunica Floarea comes to my rescue with her foul mouth. "Blood means you're ready to make children if any boy has sex with you. Got that? Men have seeds, cursed seeds, and they tell girls all kinds of lies and make all sorts of promises in order to have sex with them. Blood means you are now a grown woman. Don't worry, fancy ladies go dancing even when they bleed like this. Let me show you how to take care of yourself. Sometimes your mother is so dumb, I wonder how she will stay alive raising two girls!"

"Bunica, since we're talking about this, what shall I do about my breasts? They suddenly cover my whole chest."

"Oh, for God's sake, I'll tell your mother to take you shopping for a bra! Don't you let any boys get close to them because their hands move from place to place!"

And just like that, I am tormented, tantalized into womanhood, Mom's lesson in the signs of womanhood amounting to weeping, Bunica's making it clear that boys are involved in all this too. Loredana will get all the gory details as soon as I realize that I am not bleeding to death.

*

Mom is barely out of the bath when the guard from the police station knocks at the door. Bombonica barks at the top of her lungs. Loredana takes hold of the dog and asks the guard to wait on the veranda. He says, "Mrs. Bugan, you are called to the police station urgently so you'd better come with me." My stomach again ties up and hurts. I cannot imagine what this is about. I get Mom's bag and promise we will all wait for her right here at home. We mostly pace around the house for the two hours she is gone.

Bunica drinks some more *florio* and circles around the garden with the dog walking after her. "Goddamn little shitters, they can't just take a woman out of the bath, with her hair wet, and drag her to the police whenever they want. Oh, I am going to tell them. What can they do to an old woman like me other than to kiss her arse? Poor Mioara. Why couldn't I have normal sons, oh God?"

When Mom comes home she is radiant. "I am going to Bucureşti to see Nelu, Mother, and I need to make a package for him with food and clothing. How are we ever going to get the food? I might ask around. We need hard cheese, salami, and he wants chocolate and oranges."

"Chocolate, my arse, you tell my son. I am so happy you are going to see him! Take him some warm clothes and we'll see if we can find some hard cheese and maybe meat in lard or salt because they last for the journey." Mom's dream that she will see Dad is coming true, as true as her dream that Cătălin would be a boy. I trust all of our dreams, since Bunica Anghelina's dream about angels.

A few days later Mom is on the train with a package of clothing and the best food we could ask for from relatives and friends. When she returns, we spend half of the night talking about how she indeed saw the car and the soldier at the gate and how she walked up the stone steps to see Dad, just like in her dream. I am convinced that in great despair God offers us little moments of fast-forwarding in time so we will be reassured that life is worth the struggle. Dad is set to be tried in four months at the military tribunal in București behind closed doors and only Mom will be allowed to wait in the foyer.

Mom says that Dad looked hopeful and that when they talked he lifted up a hand, pointing to the ceiling, saying, "The world knows about us. Everything will be okay." We haven't a clue what he meant, but we are happy he is alive.

*

Bunica Floarea returns from a day trip to see Dad's sister in Tecuci with two jars of pickled green tomatoes, pickled cucumbers, corn flour, and news. She places everything on the kitchen table and starts swearing.

"You know what your shit of a grandfather Toader did to your father, he who calls himself a father to his sons? He signed a paper letting the dogs from the Securitate torture your father, he said he disowned him. Not only did he beat his sons out of the house and go to whores, now he disowns his son, the whole village knows it, they told me everywhere. The Securitate went to the house and threatened to bulldoze it if he didn't sign the paper. But what father does this to his son? What could they have done to an old man? When they asked me to do that I told them to kiss my arse! Your mother was luckier to have an adoptive father, for Neculai is a man of honor but Toader was never a father to his family."

*

Cătălin stops gaining weight, despite all the livers, carrots, and other vegetables we mash for him every day. He is still quite weak and unable to crawl properly or walk. His color is not so good either. Mom leaves her factory job indefinitely, packs Cătălin in the train with her, and heads off to the best children's hospital in Bucureşti, which is also famous for medical research. She says to Bunica, "I will only come back when my son is well. I don't need a doctor's referral or permission from the comrades at the Securitate. Mother, please look after Carmen and Loredana, and I will try to call or write as soon as I get settled into the hospital." She takes just enough clothes for her and Cătălin.

It's the end of summer. We are left at home with the microphones and fear for Cătălin, Mom, and Dad. There is a feeling of loss everywhere. I read, I read, I read, wishing to compress time into moments when my mind will go completely numb. I don't know what to talk about with anyone. Heavy with the burden of days in which I am observed, scrutinized, followed, and refused news of my parents, I write in my journal, where I can talk without being heard.

An Audience with My Father
at the Rahova Prison

My turn to experience a miracle now. I thank God for my being the firstborn child of the family. The village policeman comes asking for me one day. He says that I am to go and visit my father at the Rahova prison, where he is held for "questioning" before his trial. My cousin Fănel is to accompany me, since I am still too young to travel by myself across the country. I am happy he is coming along. He is one of my favorite cousins. I have no idea how and why this happens, but when I ask if my sister can come along, I am curtly told, "She is younger. Now, would you like to see your father?"

Sometimes you can love even an enemy!

I want to impress my father, to look sporty and strong. Perhaps he will notice how much I have changed since he drove away without telling me that we might never see each other again. It is nearing October. Flower women sell chrysanthemums the color of dirty whitewash, heavy with the first cold rains. The street corners smell of the autumn leaves piled by the wind at the foot of fences. But it's not time for coats yet, so people are wandering about in their pullovers. Over the summer I turned thirteen and I have been taking care of the house like a grown woman with responsibilities. Despite being treated like "social garbage" at school because of Dad, I feel stronger, taller, more solid in my belief that I can take the reins of suffering and keep going. Having abandoned Dumas, Malory, and Brontë, I am reading Schopenhauer (or rather about his philosophy through the poetry of Mihai Eminescu), Maupassant's stories, Dostoyevsky's *Crime and*

Punishment, Lucian Blaga's poems of the heart finding itself in the pulse of a village, and I move about gravely.

I want to tell Dad that thanks to him I feel the weights on the scales of the world: Securitate men asking questions are just Securitate men asking questions in the end. Managing without him and without Mom, and with Cătălin oscillating between living and dying, I am becoming fully equipped to speak out for the merits of cynicism. There is no revolution, no one is saved, we all crawl toward death and exploit each other on the way. I see the world for what it is, without the protection or at least the framework of my family. Ah, but there is God, and he is more often there to punish us for things we do not do, or we do not know how to fix. In vain I fall on my knees rehearsing the prostrations I learned from Bunica Anghelina: she said that God answers the honest prayers, the face level to the ground, the passion in front of the burning oil candle.

I am freakishly cheerful. As I board the train to Rahova prison in București with my cousin Fănel, I am sporting a brand-new blue running suit with white lines along the sleeves and legs. The suit is complemented by red-and-white running shoes. My skin is bright red, burned from the sun of the September and October harvest fields where my school worked on "voluntary" agricultural projects. Somehow my sports suit gives me the idea that I am an athlete running over all the obstacles in a miserable life. I imagine a stark room with a long table and chairs but no paintings save for Comrade Ceaușescu's portrait. Dad and I will sit across the table talking alone and I get to tell him what I am thinking. I want to give him a lecture on life. For the whole journey to București I am so preoccupied with my invented future conversation with Dad, I do not even notice my cousin.

*

We must first report to the Internal Ministry, an impressive place. But the only thing I feel imprinting itself in my mind, the way one thinks "I am certain I will remember this," is the fact that the guard soldier assumes I am Colonel Coman's daughter, perhaps because I so confidently demand to be taken to him.

"No, I am the daughter of Ion Bugan, but Colonel Coman wants to see me before the audience with my father."

The irony that I may look like the daughter of my father's torturer strikes me. Since I already know him, I feel strangely at ease when I see him. I take directions to the Rahova prison and double-check that there will be someone to lead me directly to my father. Now that I am inside Securitate headquarters, there is nothing more to be afraid of. It feels exactly like the times I have been so ill that there was no need to fear the doctors taking blood from me and giving me painful injections. The best thing to do is to keep the arm steady so the vein doesn't get missed—that's how I think about this visit to my father's enemies, so I might as well act as if I have nothing to fear.

*

The gates of the Rahova prison are gray, rusted, and heavier than any wall I have ever seen. They are covered in the dust of the capital's outskirts, coming from construction sites. Comrade Ceauşescu and his wife sit around every now and then and move blocks along an architectural board, shifting buildings from one side of the city to the other, building apartment blocks and demolishing churches. The city and its outskirts feel like a giant hive of bulldozers and dust. Fănel and I lean toward the small square prison window. We look for the guard. While Fănel introduces us, a terrible iron-grating sound comes from the main gate, which glides slowly on its wheels along a small track.

I peer inside the courtyard. There are dilapidated buses loaded with criminals coming out, and there are more criminals who walk into the square gray building. Everyone except the guards wears striped uniforms and hats that look like those worn by chefs. There are chains around their feet and their hands, so the noise of dragging iron mixes with the dust rising from the earth. The guards yell at the prisoners to move faster. I stand at the mouth of hell, my own mouth gaping open; dust and images coat my tongue. The thought "My father is a criminal!" jumps inside my chest, pounds, screams, and shrieks inside my throat. I taste snot and tears, and I feel hot shameful angry tears running over my face.

Fănel pulls me inside by the arms, drags me inside the prison. "Shhh, come, let's see your father, don't behave like this now!"

And suddenly I am numb, walking along corridors with heavy legs.

The reverberating sound of my father's chains on the cement floor feels like a slap on my face. We face each other through a double window with a microphone in the middle. I run to him, I want to touch him. "Please let me hug my father!"

But there is no way to get to him. His hands are tied behind his back; his prison uniform is striped like the ones I have seen in the courtyard on the other men; his head is shaved; his cheeks, thin now, look pale. My father is a broken man. He cries as I have never seen him cry. And I haven't a clue what we are saying or what Fănel is saying, other than us telling him about the food and clothing we brought for him, the socks and the shoes. All I see is his face, which toward the end of the conversation returns slowly from underneath the curtain-like tears, to the normal stubborn face of the dad I know. But the only time I am convinced he is better is when he insults me. "Carmen, you look terrible. Why are you wearing a running suit? And why are you so red?"

Half joking, half truly critical, this is his personality. Now I am hurt that he doesn't like the look I want to impress him with, and I am also happy that he is his old self. When I leave, my tears return and it feels as if they are falling on the hell where my father lives.

*

All the way to the children's hospital, where Mom is waiting with Cătălin, I cry like a child. I hold Fănel's hand and shiver. He is crying too. He is one of Tanti Săftica's sons who helped raise Loredana and me when we were little. I always loved him because he brought us candy with a soft strawberry core and danced *hora* in the kitchen with me and Loredana, teaching us the steps. My father's red eyes burning in his face, his untold pain, are the only things I see. Fănel has to hold me steady when we cross the streets. "Let's find some water to wash our faces. Your mom will be embarrassed to see we're behaving like this."

Mom's face looks bony. She has been sleeping on a hospital chair for weeks, watching over Cătălin like a hawk, ready at any minute to take him in her arms and run after the doctors. Cătălin is still small, but pink-looking now, all wrapped up in white. I sob again, this time in Mom's arms, and it feels so good I don't want to stop or to leave her. Fănel takes my brother in his arms, kisses him, and talks to him in baby language. We do this until everyone quiets down, then I sit in Mom's chair holding Cătălin. His body feels soft, comforting, small, warm. His little hands grab at my nose and travel across my cheeks. I am afraid to squeeze him too hard so I kiss him and kiss his smiles. He makes *goooh* and *eeehhhh* sounds.

"Dad is okay, Mom. He even insulted me, he told me I look ugly in my running suit, so don't worry. We brought him his heavy lamb skin coat, changes of socks and underwear, his shoes, and some fried chicken with bread and cheese. Bunica and Loredana are well, too. How is Cătuță? When are you coming home?"

"We found out that he was given excessive amounts of antibiotics in the hospital in Galați and his body became weak from it. They are running some more tests and we need to continue a strong diet for him. But he will live and he will be all right. It may be another month before we can come home. How are you doing at home for food?" As she says this, Mom looks spent. Yet she tries to smile, to *smile* for me, in this room with rusted children's beds, where she lives at the edge of endurance.

"Don't worry, Mom. Tanti Săftica and Tanti Mariana feed us, and Nenea Titi also leaves cheese and salami for us, and we have the milk from Bunicu, the flour too. Trust me, we're okay. But we miss you. Loredana wanted to come along, but the Securitate didn't let her. She said to tell you that now she can make good bean soup and polenta and can't wait to cook for you and Cătălin when you come home. And Bunica still swears a lot, which is a good sign."

Now I try to smile for her, to make her believe that we are surviving.

It's hard to say goodbye to Mom and Cătălin, to leave them among white iron cots and white chairs, stained with rust, stained baby sheets and blankets, hoping and taking medication in the white room that smells of iodine, alcohol, baby pee, and antibiotics. But this day is better than many I have lived through in the past few months and I have to go home to bring news to Loredana and Bunica.

*

Late November now and one day the sound of shuffling leaves comes through the window with my mother's voice. "Look, Cătuță, we're back at home now."

I throw Flaubert on the floor with a huge thump and run to them. Loredana and Bunica Floarea are so thrilled that they smother Mom and Cătălin before I manage to get to them.

We plan to make them a good meal in the evening. We'll kill a hen, make a strong broth with potatoes and carrots, and then fry the meat with garlic and polenta. Because there is no man in the house to cut the throat of the hen, I do it. It's a bloody thing. The head goes with white eyes on one side of the yard, the body leaps all over the dead leaves, bleeding, and I am left with the murderous knife in my hands. But as I pluck the feathers in hot water and clean the bird, I am grateful that we will have a meal to celebrate Mom's return, so I say a quick Our Father in my mind to absolve myself of the sin of slitting the hen's throat. I feel more of a man these days; I deal in life and death. The aromas of food fill the house, making Mom's return truly comforting. If we weren't so tired and so depressed, I would grab Mom and Loredana and Bunica by the hands and make them dance in the middle of the yard with me.

"Nelu's trial is coming in a week or so and I will go. I will not be allowed to speak with him or to attend the trial, but I will stay in the waiting room at least to see him go in and come out. I was told also that as soon as I return from the trial, they will come to take the seals off the doors, so we can go into the rest of the house. Girls, there will be so much work to do, all these months with everything piled on the floor. But we'll dust it all carefully and put the photos and the tapestries back on the walls, make the house look good for Christmas, no?"

When she comes back with the verdict of the judge, "ten years in prison for propaganda against the socialist regime," we accept it without any questions. As they had told her, she only saw him going into and out of the room. He is incarcerated at Aiud, the harshest prison in the country. Again, seeing him alive is more important than the heavy, long condemnation to which we are all subjected: us with waiting, him with God knows what tortures.

Mom is cheerful and I suspect it doesn't have to do with the warm fire Bunica is keeping up this evening in the kitchen, or with the Securitate giving us access to the house again. I know it is because Cătălin finally holds his neck up firmly and crawls. I don't even think that at this moment she is as worried about Dad as she used to be; neither am I, truth be told. Now Cătălin has his moment and to prove he is the center of attention, he crawls to the opened cupboard and drags out a plastic bag with a few eggs in it, falls over it, smashes the eggs, and laughs at the yolks running all over the rug, all over his clothing. His laughter is crystal bells ringing innocent happiness into the ears of the microphones set in the curtain rods.

*

The first Christmas without Dad is here. I know this is another of those times I will remember for the rest of my life. We want to do everything for Cătălin, as everything right and celebratory was done for us. Loredana takes out the tree decorations, the lights, the red and green sparkly garlands. But these are the decorations Dad bought years ago, the lights he made turn on one after the other in sequence, so we could enjoy bursts of color. Mom comes home dragging a tree off the bus, leaving a clean trail on the street snow. Usually Mom and Dad would come home with the tree strapped to the top of the car. I make mayonnaise. I have been beating the egg yolks, lemon, mustard, and sunflower oil with two forks for two hours and my arm is about to swell. Last time we were all together, Mom made the mayonnaise and Dad encouraged her from his chair, drinking wine and singing with Loredana and me. And before she had a chance to mix the mayonnaise with the vegetables and chicken, Dad ate half of it; he laughed and said he just had to taste it, so Mom had to work twice as hard to make more. Loredana beats the egg whites with sugar and vanilla powder to make meringue. Bunica roasts the chicken and potatoes, but we also got pork meat from Tanti Săftica, and sausages, so we're making stuffed vine leaves in tomato sauce. The house smells like vanilla and cottage cheese from Titi.

We don't mention Dad's absence, but I notice that when lumps come to our throats, we just work harder. We have cleaned the house furiously, washing and polishing every door, doorknob, and window, taking the rugs from the hall and veranda out on the snow and airing them. In the kitchen, where the rug gets worn more, we lay a fresh clean one that matches the color of the bedspreads. I split so much wood that I feel like Tolstoy declaiming the importance of physical labor. The fire roars. The carolers, Securitate or not, still come to the door to sing to us, with Bombonica in tow, barking. This is the only music we listen to this Christmas. No one turns on the radio anymore. I am not sure if this is a secret conspiracy not to remind ourselves of Dad, who turns on a radio in every part of the house he happens to be in, or if we feel that listening to music is an affront to his absence. In a lot of ways we behave like a family experiencing a very long funeral when only keening or speaking is proper. It's a relief to see Bunicu Neculai arrive, and Tanti Săftica with her four sons and their families. Only Bunicu and Tanti Săftica want to go to church on Christmas Day; the rest want to celebrate on Christmas Eve and sleep in the morning. Loredana is Santa Claus for my brother. She is all decked out in her red mantle and mask, her decorated cane and her bag of presents so sparkly that not even Bombonica recognizes her.

We have done our best to prepare for this Christmas, and Cătălin has received his colorful toys by the tree. The government has even allowed us to keep the electricity on all night, and there are red, green, blue, orange, and yellow lights that set the silver garland shining in the hall. But as we sit around the table to eat, Mom's voice breaks down. "I wonder what Nelu is doing tonight."

And just like that, the women start crying, the men get teary-eyed and try to hush them, and I go with Loredana and Cătălin by the tree, to stuff ourselves with candy, to stop the tears.

"Even if he stays in prison ten more years and comes home old and ill, it would still be a blessing to have him back," I hear Mom say.

I want to rush to her and scream, "Stop crying. Dad told me I will even eat fire—that's all he had to say to me the night he left!"

But I cannot do that because I miss him too and I wonder what kind of Christmas he might have in his prison cell. I know that his crime consists of nothing other than asking for food and dignity for our godforsaken country. Without someone like him, what are we all? Mom cries loud enough to break even the hearts of the walls.

Loredana makes a little airplane of Cătălin, lifting him up on her hands, and glides him toward the tree. She goes "oueeee" and he giggles; she passes him up to me, and I go "oueeee" and he giggles. Just like that, it is the end of 1983. I wonder if the Chinese man is playing with his children tonight or if he will brag about hearing us play by the tree, when he next gets drunk at the vet's house. Or maybe he will wait until the new year to change the tapes or to check the microphones. I will remember this as the most stifled Christmas in my life, for the lump in my throat doesn't really go away with candy, with food, with carols, or with playing with Cătălin.

My Parents' Divorce

Mariana, who is a nurse, spends her time when she is at home smoking cigarettes and reading. All over the house and on top of opened books you can see small porcelain cups of Turkish coffee caked with coffee grounds and sugar. Clean and dirty shirts, trousers, winter coats are mixed on the floor and in corners. Inside her huge oak closets, in place of clothes, there are books in disorderly, tall piles. When I go over, she sits around talking to Mom and I walk into the closets looking for books. I am fourteen and still reading voraciously: Balzac, Flaubert, Zola, Maupassant, Dostoyevsky, Sadoveanu, Eminescu, Tolstoy. I ask Mariana for romantic stories and she gives me romantic novels. When I feel like reading science fiction, she gives me science fiction. I want travel novels—"novels to take me far from here"—and she says, "Rouen, Paris, the Himalayas, where do you want to go?" And she covers me in books. No one cares if *Nana, Bel Ami,* or *Anna Karenina* might be a bit too intense for my age. Mariana's closet library and lending policy embody democracy. I love the books that come in many volumes and that zoom in and stop time in one room, on one face, one event, because the pleasure lasts longer. When the electricity is left on by the government I read straight through the night while Cătălin sleeps nestled in the crook of my arm and Mom makes sweaters at her knitting machine, drinking Ness instant coffee foamed with a bit of water and coarse sugar first and then diluted with hot water. The Securitate man changes his tapes around the garage, Mom goes to her weekly interrogations in Tecuci, the policemen make their rounds at the house to see if we are contacted by American spies, and, when I stop doing housework, I read.

I am head in the closet feet outside and I half-listen, absentmindedly, to Mariana and Mom. Mom cries softly. "Mariana, I was told to divorce Nelu. Carmen was rejected by the entrance examiners at high school, they are sending Loredana back from school, and they told me that Cătălin will not be allowed to begin kindergarten unless I divorce Nelu publicly, to show that I do not agree with his politics."

I didn't know that Mom had had this conversation with the Securitate. I listen attentively now, standing bent over the pile of books.

"They told me I will be fired from the willow basket factory. I need to feed the kids, but Nelu will think the worst of it."

I come out of the closet and sit on the floor next to Mariana and Mom. *Divorce* is such a strange word. It's like saying someone abused you, cheated on you. It just doesn't happen around here, even if your husband beats you every day and sleeps with other women.

"But if you divorce, can we see Dad?" I ask, since we haven't seen him for ages now and we really don't know if he is still alive.

"I know a lawyer who can advise you on this, but we have to figure out a way to meet him without the Securitate knowing," offers Mariana.

Mom says she'll talk it over with her sister Balaşa and her husband, Dan, who also might know someone who can advise. The words the Securitate said to Mom, "you mustn't pollute your children's minds by staying married to your husband," imprint themselves on my mind for years to come. I feel we are branded like criminals or like collective cows with numbers burned onto their skin: "polluted."

*

It's autumn and the grapes in our vine tunnel hang heavy with red-black juice. Leaves are beginning to burn. I spend some afternoons playing my guitar on the porch and the neighbors clap from their yards. In happier times we would think about helping Bunicu make his wine. In happier times there would be an accordion at Bunicu's

house, we'd sit around tapping our feet to the music, and I'd be thinking, "*Mină caii,* Neculai." In happier times Dad would say, "Better go
to the mountains for a weekend before it gets cold." I miss my father.
Uncle Dan is an artisan, so he placed a photo of Dad in a wooden
frame decorated with etchings of vine leaves and grapes. Dad wears
a white shirt unbuttoned at the neck. He must be in his early forties,
truly handsome. This is my favorite picture of all we have. His face
looks young, he still has most of his hair, he smiles gently (which is
uncharacteristic of him), and he seems truly relaxed (which is also
almost impossible for him). I feel time passing painfully without our
getting to know each other: father, daughter, family. Somewhere in
the Aiud prison his chains must be dragging with their awful iron
sound on cement and he doesn't know how I love him.

I want to explain to him that growing up without a father, I have
to fend for myself, be my own shield, build a kind of hardness around
me. Somewhere deep inside I wish that the night he left I had ham-
mered nails in his tires as I had threatened and kept him home. I
resent how he left me and I yearn to argue with him, face-to-face.

This week a Securitate man told Bunica Floarea again that Dad
stabbed and killed himself in prison with the sharpened handle of a
spoon.

"You disrespectful, wretched kid, you could be my own son. How
dare you say my son would think of something as stupid as to kill
himself?"

She sends him away and then turns to me, looking straight into
my eyes: "Don't let them intimidate you!"

I know that I can just about hold my ground from now on when
they come for interrogations. When Bunica is like this, I love her. We
laugh with a mad triumphant laugh. Maybe the divorce is not a bad
idea, maybe we can see Dad in flesh and blood.

The story of the spoon makes me sick to my stomach. I want to put
this pain in a poem along with my feelings of futility, with gratitude
for my happy childhood, with words of encouragement and belief in
him, with his image in the grape-framed photo in which he doesn't

know yet about Aiud. Mostly I want the poem to take this homesick-ness for Dad's arms from me, from Loredana, and from Mom. I take the photo from the hallway wall to the grape trellis and I sit on cement writing in quatrains. Mom finds me when she comes from work. I read the poem to her and Loredana, who says, "He is so alive here, it's like having him in front of me."

Mom cries and cries.

Loredana doesn't cry, but her face speaks of pain—pain she keeps to herself until moments like this.

By the time we go to bed, the poem returns my dad to us. From this moment on I never stop writing poetry, though I have to burn the poems that mention prison so the Securitate don't find them. Poems come and go like that—moments painted in images that in turn be-come their own reality mixed with the actual memory of Dad so that sometimes we remember my re-creation of Dad, not him; we idealize him because of his absence. But it's not important that the poems stay or go: I discover a way to alleviate our family's suffering even though when I read the poems to Mom and my sister it seems that I create more pain at first. Mom loves words, loves explanations of feelings to negotiate pain, and I can provide this for her. My sister says her feelings are exteriorized, articulated by the emotions in the poem, and I can help bring things out.

"There is a date for divorce," Mom says, "in a couple of weeks."

*

At the Aiud prison the guard opens the small square window in the wall of my father's cell. "Bugan, to the interrogation room."

Dad is given a glass of buttermilk and is told that Mom has filed for divorce.

"We want you to write down the reason for which you think your wife wants to divorce you. Clearly she must be tired of being alone. See, even she abandons you."

The guard leaves him alone in the room. Dad hasn't seen buttermilk in at least two years so he assumes the milk is poisoned. He pours the contents of the glass, little by little, into the mouth of the small fireplace while the guard is away. There is nothing he can think of and he writes, "My wife and I always were committed to each other and I find no reason why she herself will want to divorce me. Ion Bugan."

The guard returns to the room. On the table he places three red apples and informs Dad that Mom sent them to him. Dad reads the symbolism: he has three children, so Mom must be telling him that now he is losing his children. It is true she always fought with him about his manifestos, about the risks he was putting our family under, about his selfishness to think that it's all right to sacrifice his family for a pointless political ideal. He remembers the fights, the sleepless nights at the typewriter, her hatred at leaving the children, his heart pounding when the police came time and again to check the typewriter. He almost believes that perhaps she sent the apples and he drags the chains around his ankles back to the cell carrying them in his hands. He places the apples on the bed and doesn't eat them.

*

It's seven in the morning sometime in November 1985. Dad is being brought from Aiud to Tecuci, a two-day drive, meaning he was in prison in Galați last night. At the bus station, Loredana, Mom, Cătălin, Bunica Floarea, and I meet Bunicu Neculai. We get off at the city center roundabout and head toward the courthouse. I hold Cătălin, who is two and a half years old. Loredana, Bunicu, and I pass Cătălin around. I think all of us need the warmth of the child in our arms. We need stability against this day. When we arrive at the courthouse there are people strewn about the yard waiting for the windowless prison van to arrive. No one knows how the news got around, but the whole town and the whole village know my father will be here this morning, and when the van slows down at the courthouse gates, people begin chanting, *"Bugan, Bugan, Bugan, Bugan."* I am pretty sure they don't really know the Securitate, since they make these stupid, risky gestures. They chant slowly, whisperingly, clearly. I am scared and I am hypnotized. We all hold each other, Mom, Loredana, Cătălin, Bunicu Neculai, Bunica Floarea.

Dad is brought out tied to another man by his handcuffs. His uniform is striped, gray, he has a cap on his head and he blinks in the light.

"Tăticu, Tăticu," I say with Loredana, calling for him.

He sees us and all of us freeze for the second before he is pushed inside, bare feet in brown shoes, with heavy chains around his ankles. He disappears inside with my breath. For the next while we wait. And then there is one finger, one finger through the grates of the top-floor window and people start chanting again, louder, encouraged by seeing him: *"Bugan, Bugan, Bugan."*

This time I am proud of my father and I want to say, "I am his daughter, you can ask *me* about him! No one can do what he did."

Mom whispers between her tears, "Nelu is alive."

Bunica Floarea says, "My boy's alive, that's my boy."

Bunicu Neculai says, "Dear God, the boy's with us, thank God."

Loredana, Cătălin, and I are not allowed to go inside the courtroom, but a nice woman leaves the door slightly cracked—just a centimeter—so that we can get a glimpse of Dad. I only see his feet in the brown shoes and I can hear the small sound of chains on the floor as he shuffles his feet. Everyone else is inside. It's cold and the steam from our breath rises to the ceiling and goes through the crack in the door.

At the end of the divorce proceedings I hear Dad stand to ask the judge if he may see his children, please. We freeze in the opened door until Mom says, "Carmen, wouldn't you like to go to Dad to say hello?"

I rush to his arms and bury my head in his chest. Time halts and freezes. My homesickness for him becomes so profound that I cling to him as if I am another arm. I can't make space for Loredana and Cătălin, who also stick to Dad like orange skins before you peel them from the fruit. I want to cover Dad up, to make him invisible, to absorb him into our bodies—Loredana's, Cătălin's, and mine—and take him home, oh good God, take my daddy home. The judge weeps and leaves the room. It takes two policemen to unstick my sister, my brother, and me from my dad's body, limb by limb, cheek by tear-soaked cheek, finger by clutched finger. By the time Mom and my grandparents go, I am already numb with pain and new longing for Dad's arms. Then it's all only very cold air in the street. I see no one, I hear nothing, I walk along and I walk along and I keep on walking.

I don't know how I arrive home and where everyone is, but when I come to the grape tunnel they are there saying they don't remember how they arrived home either and more importantly who held on to Cătălin, who is also, miraculously, home. Mom begins cleaning the kitchen windows. She hands me newspapers. "You clean this porch window."

I breathe on the window. On my breath I write "Dad." I breathe again on the window and I write the first line about the divorce, which was an oath of love. Mom sees me and says, "Here's a pencil and paper."

I write the poem and one by one we read it, not aloud. It rhymes and it spells in quatrains that divorce in our case is really all about love. The first and last stanzas read like this:

Unde eşti tăticule?
Lacrimile-mi curg şiroaie.
De ce-ai plecat tată,
Ai lăsat in urmă furtuni si ploaie?

Sărută-ne tata
Sărută-ne pe noi
Că nu se ştie niciodată
Cînd vom ieşi din noroi.

Daddy, where are you?
My tears flow and flow.

Father, why did you leave us
Inside thunderstorms?

Now kiss us, Father,
Bless us with kisses
For we do not know when
We will come out of this mud.

Dad is alive, after all. The following week we find out we can go back
to school, this time officially fatherless.

*

In the coming months I develop sleeplessness and migraine head-
aches. I have nightly dreams in which the devil dressed in red clothes
hemmed with gold waits for me to turn in bed and strikes me in the
head with an iron hatchet. I cannot handle light, I am nauseated, and
when I get any relief, I go walking for many hours and for many
miles. Mom says sometimes people find me walking in the fields in
the next village over and bring me home. I don't remember any of
this but many times I feel the familiar rush of cold air on my face and
I love the freedom of the wind. At night, when I can, I continue to
read with Cătălin next to me while Mom drinks her coffee and knits
sweaters. On payday she and I sit in the middle of the bed making a
pile of banknotes for each bill, and we plan the foods we need to trade
sweaters and knitted hats for. Between Mom and me the house is running; we always know where the others are and who is looking after
Cătălin. The Securitate guard still follows me to school every day but
by now I am used to him.

My mother and I become one soul torn between two bodies: we
read each other's moods. Loredana and I are each other's shadows,
but I am the one who speaks more and she is the one who bends over
the washing and the cooking silently. None of us gets sleep, and the
migraines clench my head in iron bars and squeeze my skull until I
see stars. I have dreams in which I run away far from here, where there

are fresh green grass fields and the clouds are all puffy and happy in the sky. I run inside Bunica Anghelina's dream with all the angels to the place of no pain where it doesn't rain but a gentle breeze brings with it their music.

*

And then it's spring and there is a postcard from my father: "I am fifty. Make a cake for me." We make a cake for him and place the postcard from prison on the table next to it.

*

I am angry. Since I was twelve my life has been lived in public, scrutinized, reviewed, pondered, and recorded over and over again. The guard who follows me to school and oversees the recordings of my family continues to brag, "I can hear the child breathing and crying."

He always tells neighbors about this as if he really wants us to know it. This sentence is becoming a refrain. We are still asked (and comply with the order) to keep the curtains open at all times so the guards can see what happens in the house from the churchyard. The Securitate men have also settled in the church bell tower; the teachers from school see them taking shifts. Day and night I can hear the thump of a guard jumping the fence between the church and the back of our house.

I am angry with God because he sends me the dreams of the devil with the hatchet aiming for my throat every time I am about to fall asleep. I am angry because he gave people imagination to paint frescoes of idyllic godly beauty on the outside church walls and he also gave Securitate the imagination and the patience to treat me and my family as if we were animals in a kennel. I still sleep mostly in my clothes, still don't feel secure enough to wear pajamas. In the middle of the night Securitate people unlock the front door of the house I helped to build and they sit in the living room. Bunica Floarea, my mother, my brother, my sister, and I feign sleeping: we breathe shallow breaths under the sheets. We all share the same bed now, fully clothed, like sardines in a metal can, packed in our vinegar sweat. I look at our icon of Saint Mary, at the burning oil candle under it, and seek solace, knowing it is people who do this to us, not God.

If we want to say something about my father, we write it on a piece of paper, pass the note around silently, read it, and burn it. We use layers of subtext, so "make the fire" may mean "I have something to say that we need to burn." The neighbors are asked to inform on us and they do—they have no choice. But they also write to us, on small pieces of paper, "I was told to ask you the following question." When I take my baths they are rushed and not in the bathtub. I wash in a small basin in the bathroom, quickly, careful to undress only the parts I wash. We never lock the door when we go somewhere; we joke that our house is the safest one in România since it is so heavily guarded.

While my exterior life is recorded and publicly scrutinized, I have an internal life that allows me to survive. I return to Mariana's closets like a beggar, like a penitent sufferer who has not sinned, like a woman desperate to stick a fist in the face of the sky and tear a hole in the universe through which to escape. Mariana loads my bag with books and I set off on trails of honest friendships, of unlying love, mountain passes where the road is absorbed into the sky. I cannot breathe unless I read about the horizon, or the blue oceans, or unless the altitude of the mountain crossing is very high. I get dizzy looking back or down. I have developed tachycardia, the doctor in Tecuci says. I have become a desperate reader. Blaga and Eminescu give me emotions I want to reach through the utter discipline of the verse. I imitate Eminescu's poetry in my own writing. But in my poetry I want to shatter the sound of my father's chains, I want to crush the microphones under my feet and make beauty with them, transform them. I am thinking, "You can make me suffer but I will make you cry for all the beauty I create, for the pity of it."

There is the peach tree my father and I planted before he left. This year it puts forth its first peaches, which have no consciousness of how they came into existence or of what happens around the house while they soak up the rain and sun and grow. I write a poem about the peaches. Then there are the dahlias growing wildly for no one. Not even families who need them for their dead stop at our house on their way to the cemetery to collect them. So I write poems about the yellow dahlias—the free dahlias that don't know there is a war raging in the house, between us and the listening walls.

"Walls have ears, walls have ears, walls have ears," we keep writing to each other. "Be careful, walls have ears."

I take dahlias to the grave of Bunica Anghelina, where I light incense and candles, and speak aloud about my anger. "*Mină caii, Neculai*," I say to her blue peeling cross.

I feel like the chick that convulsed in our hands before it finished fighting with the toothless hag. But every day I decide I am not the chick and I will put my fist in the face of suffering, both angry fists if I have to. I will win, I will grow, I am so much stronger than a victim.

Aiud

I carry Cătălin under my right arm across the train tracks at the Aiud railway station. There are plastic bags stuffed with food and clothes in my left hand. The place is so crowded that people have spilled onto the tracks, bringing the train traffic to a standstill. Many of them are carrying packages and suitcases, so it dawns on me that lots of them are here for the same reason as us. It took us two and a half days to get here from Tecuci, so we are truly exhausted. I feel nauseated from the halting and starting of the trains at each station. Loredana and Mom stagger under suitcases and bags, and Mom yells at me not to drop Cătălin, but soon we all break into laughter because Cătălin thinks I am playing airplane with him and makes wings of his arms, giggling, "Zzzooooooom, ooueee, zzhoooom."

"You're my airplane lamb," I say to him. "Hang in there, Cătuță!" He doesn't know we are going to prison to visit Dad. He thinks we are going to see Dad in the faraway place where he "works" and from which "he will come home one day."

Loredana is in charge of asking for directions to the nearest hotel, where we are to drop off the luggage, and she finds a two-star place almost right away. There is a sink in the room. The bathroom and shower are down the hall, but we are told that there is no electricity so there isn't hot water.

"Actually," the lady says, "sorry, dear, but the water is already switched off for the day, so if you need drinking water get some from a café for the night."

We are used to this as it's the same in Tecuci: water off half a day, electricity off in the evenings and, sometimes, just off for days. We are grateful that Bunicu Neculai buys the candles at church and brings them to us instead of lighting them for the dead in our family.

"Well, at least a place to put our heads down," Mom says as she pays the lady. "We'll be tired anyway by the evening."

The prison is right in the city. You cannot miss it. It is surrounded by ancient walls so it feels like a Roman fortress with its tiny windows covered in iron grates. Police direct the crowd of visitors to the triage area. On top of the wall there is a tall barbed wire fence to stop prisoners from escaping. A big iron gate opens every once in a while and I see the trucks loaded with criminals either going to or coming from their labor camps, wherever they are. The walls around the complex of prison buildings seem circular, so we walk around them until we find the right window. It's never ending. You cannot hide yourself from onlookers when you walk in a circle: you cannot hide behind a corner and pretend you are just crossing the street on which the prison happens to be located. I feel we are stuck on the roundabout sidewalk where only prison visitors go. I am humiliated.

Loredana and Mom have no trouble speaking to the man at the small window in the stone wall. They ask where to report for an appointment to see a prisoner today.

"How many are you?" he asks.

"Four," Mom says, "me—the wife—and the three children."

After Mom shows him the appointment letter, the jail policeman directs us to the visitors' waiting room, which is around the wall, where the *VORBITOR* sign is.

I can think of a million places where we could visit Dad—at the store in Iveşti where he feeds the hungry people, at his TV repair shop where he fixes things for people, at our new house where he makes every inch of land beautiful with his hands, but not here. I am sixteen now and want to be proud of my father, as I was at the Black Sea when he swam with Loredana and me on his back, so far out Mom was screaming from the shore. Or the dad who held me by my right hand at Sinaia when I wanted to peer down into the mountain gorge from a cliff and he thought I was courageous, adventurous. That surely got him into a fight with Mom, but I trusted his hand holding mine the way I trusted the air in my lungs, and I hung over the precipice looking down over the heads of the pine trees and went "Ehhhh—heeeeeh, Daddy, this is sooo awesome!" Then he was the strongest dad in the whole universe. And now he is a prisoner who lives with chains around his ankles and who must obey the guards who abuse him. But no one has time or can understand my feelings. Either way I never bother to talk about this with Mom and Loredana because I already know their response. I grab little Cătălin with one hand, part of the food we brought for Dad with the other, and I follow my family holding my head high, making up imaginary conversations with people looking at us.

In the waiting room there are wooden benches so packed with families that people take turns sitting and standing. The smell of sweat, train, deep-fried meats, and unwashed feet nauseates me. Instinctively I look around to compare our family with others. I analyze their clothes to see who comes from the city and who wears homemade dresses and shirts, who smells like a farm and who smells like cheap perfume, who wears high heels and who wears the brown flat shoes one wears to work in a factory. I try to guess the crimes of the prisoners by the look of their families: Did they steal because of poverty? Did they rebel, like my father, because they had enough leisure time to plan a protest? Were they so frustrated in the bread line they swore at Ceauşescu and got arrested? The lines, the waiting lines to register for the visits, are long. Mom finds out that there were people there from eight in the morning and almost nothing moved. Now it's four in the afternoon, but we must wait at least to be given a ticket number so that tomorrow we can be distinguished from the new herd of visitors. I read my book, I play with Cătălin. Mom and Loredana talk to people switching places on the benches and they find out all kinds of stuff that drifts in and out of my awareness.

"What's your husband in for?" asks an old lady.

"He demonstrated in Bucureşti in '83," Mom says, and the lady brightens up.

"The man with the red car and the placard?"

"Yes."

"Ohh . . . he is still alive?" asks the lady.

"Thankfully."

Everyone, wherever we go and introduce ourselves by our last name, knows who we are. I am used to this kind of "fame" now. I crave anonymity. I wish someone would ask me my name and then say, "Oh, I don't know this name. It's nice to meet you."

And I am nervous about seeing Dad, partly because I want to support him, partly because I want to reproach him for branding my name like this without asking me if I wanted to be known for his troubles with the government. I remember how he cried quietly when I saw him at the Rahova prison in 1983. I am afraid of his pain, of his tears, because I cannot do anything to make them go away. But it's already six and I am woken from my thoughts by the bell sending us back into the street.

"No more audiences today," the guard announces.

*

It's now night and we've gone to sleep in the hotel room. Something—a bug—bites under my shirt and I scratch.

"Mom, something bit me," I call out.

"Me too," Loredana announces, annoyed.

"It must be lice or ticks or something," Mom suggests.

Cătălin has to pee and I go with him. Mom and Loredana stumble over each other and shake out the sheets. It doesn't work. We laugh so hard at the noises we make when we are bitten that we cry.

*

In the morning we take turns washing at the basin in the room. We change clothes. Once Cătălin is dressed, we make an inventory of the food we brought for Dad and the leftovers we have for ourselves. It's now the third day and the bread is stale, going green at the corners.

"If we cut the corners, there's still a chance," I say.

The salami still stands. The tomatoes are soft and gone. The deep-fried chicken drumsticks for Dad are still not smelly but we doubt they'll last for another day so we offer Cătălin one, because he is clearly hungry.

"But we brought this for Daddy, so I will keep it for him," he says.

It's hard to explain the feeling this stirs in me. When we packed the swiss cheese at home for Dad, Mom saw Cătălin salivate and she wanted to give him some. He looked at her and said, "For Daddy—I don't want it." There is goodness in my brother that I have never known in anyone else. Growing up as he is in this deprivation, he is developing a kind of generosity that is like water poured down a scorched throat. Cătălin is too young for such generosity.

*

"Bugan family, to the interview," the guard yells over the crowd in the waiting room. Mom and Loredana, who have been chatting with yesterday's acquaintances, stand and shake hands with them

"Good luck."

"Good luck to you. May you find your husband well."

Then we grab the food package for Dad and our little day bag.

"You divorced him," says the guard to my mother. "Why are you here?"

"My *husband* still has three children and I want to be there when they see their father."

Mom enunciates the word *husband* to make the guard understand that the divorce was a sham and she will treat it as such. She stands her ground firmly and waits. I have Cătălin in my arms. We follow the guard through many rooms, a courtyard, other rooms, so that I no longer know where I am. Doors have been locked and chained behind us. I feel as if thick hands are wrapped around my throat, squeezing it. We are led into a glass room with glass booths and backless chairs in front of each. There is a microphone in each booth, lodged inside the wall dividing the room into the side of the convicts and the side of the visitors.

"You have to speak loudly and clearly," the guard says, "into the microphone." And, "You are only allowed to talk about the health of the family."

We are given twenty minutes. There are no other visitors here. Once the guard checks the clock, we hear chains being dragged on cement and the rumble of keys.

My father approaches slowly. They direct him to sit down on his chair on the other side of the booth and he complies, intimidated, like a child at school, afraid of breaking the rules. All my life I saw him in charge of people, but not since he was arrested and certainly not now. He wears the same striped gray uniform and the same gray cap he wore at the divorce. The guard watches us. My father fixes his gaze on all of us at once, intensely, as if he wants to take all of us into his eyes at the same time. Then his face clouds over and tears fill his eye-light, streaming on his face like rain on a window. I don't see the others in my family, just him. My own tears make his face dance behind the glass wall. I cannot touch him, I am aware of this. Once again, I want to put my fist in the face of the universe and break a hole in it. But this time I do not seek escape. This time I want to pound the hole through which I can travel to my father who is so far away behind the glass, behind his crying. A long time passes. An eternity passes.

Mom breaks out in loud sobs and asks Dad, "Nelu, *dar nu vrei să ne spui nimic?*"—Don't you want to say anything to us?

And then Cătălin quickly says, "*Tăticu, ți-am adus niște mîncare.*"— Daddy, I brought you some food.

"Cătăline, *da tu ce mai faci, băiatul lui tata?*" (Cătăline, my boy, how are you?) asks Dad of Cătălin, and Cătălin says, "*Bine.*" (Fine.)

The rest I don't remember. We must have talked about Bunica Floarea, Bunicu Neculai, Titi, Tanti Săftica. When the guard orders

Dad to leave, says visiting time is over, I say to Dad, "You look after
yourself, Daddy. I will take care of the rest at home."

I want to be in control. I want to show him that I am his oldest and bravest child who will figure everything out, take care of my
mother for him, and look after Cătălin and Loredana. But the truth
is that we all take care of each other and that Cătălin, with his innocence, his laughter, his generosity, saves us from despair every day.

I don't know how we get back to the hotel but we cry there in
style, we indulge in crying until our hearts are spilled out all over
the lice-infested beds. And then we take turns washing our faces at
the basin and head for the train station, me with my "airplane lamb"
under my right arm.

*

From here we are going to the Black Sea. It's August. Mom has already planned on visiting her brother Ştefan in Constanța. He works
on an oil rig out in the deep waters but in a few days he will return to
shore for his two weeks to be with his wife and our three cousins. I
will finally see my beloved sea, which I have missed so much. I have
pleaded with Mom for a trip there since last summer. The train that
takes us away from Aiud goes slowly and stops at each village station,
crossing over rivers, roads, dirt streets, mountains, going through tun-
nels, coming to the other side slowly, slowly like Bunicu Neculai's
cart, whistling. It gives me time to distance myself from the prison
visit and slowly work my way outward into the landscape, where I can
breathe. Time to emerge little by little, not rush, out of the darkness
where my father remains. "*Mînă caii*, Neculai," I murmur to myself,
thinking of the journey ahead, toward the sea. I am grateful for the
heat I feel from the summer sun. I am grateful that there are no chains
around my ankles as I rub my feet with a mixture of fear and relief. I
am especially grateful that I am back on the road, so I stick my head
out of the compartment window, close my eyes, and let the wind touch
my face.

My eyes burn from crying. My father doesn't sweat from the sun;

he is not on the road somewhere. At each station I count the number of villages adding up between me and him. This is the price of asking for freedom in my country. This is what you have to endure just for asking to be free to speak. And the worst part is that all this suffering is in vain, nothing will change. Ceauşescu makes speeches at the congresses announcing unparalleled progress in technology, industry, and agriculture; his wife is given prizes for fake "leading science discoveries in chemistry"; the stores are absolutely empty and dark; the crops, if they don't fail, go straight to Russia on big freight trains, as our electricity goes there, for free. A cold war is raging and we are feeding the Russians. And because our ration cards are meant to be collected only from Tecuci, we are not able to buy bread from bakeries on this side of the country, but have to limit ourselves to bagels, when they happen to be there as we pass by.

We are now in Bucureşti. The train for Constanţa is getting excessively busy with people going to the sea. We stand for the whole journey as there isn't even enough space to move so that people can take turns standing and sitting. Passengers just droop their heads like wilted plants and drowse on one another with the kind of senseless familiarity developed from traveling in cramped public transport. It's night. When we arrive we take a taxi to my uncle's place and collapse before getting a chance to shower, eat, or drink.

*

In the morning, in Constanţa, Loredana and Mom are already up and speaking with my uncle's family, setting up breakfast, telling them about the visit to my father in prison. Cătălin sticks his fingers in my eyes and then pulls at my hair. I do not listen or even hear all the niceties being uttered—all I care for is the sea.

You can smell the sea in the bus that goes from the city center to the beach because it is always packed with people smelling of suntan lotion, sand, and salt. I run into the water while everyone unpacks and I scream to the incoming tide, "I am glad to find you well, my sea!" The hair on my arms stands; there is happiness waiting to come out and I am greedy to breathe in the salty spray. In my mind I tell Dad that we have arrived at the sea and it's beautiful. I run into the waves that come to greet me with cold, strong arms. I am now salty; I would love to be a heroine from a novel set in Greece or the south of France. No, I would rather be a man who crosses the sea on a plank of wood and spends nights gazing at plankton and stars all mixing up at the close horizon made by giant waves. No, maybe I want to be a violinist walking at the edge of the sea looking at red and blue boats heavy with fish and rusted nets, thinking about putting the images of the small harbor into music. *Whoooshh, whooossh, whuuuush, whoosh, whoosh.* Gold, warm, soft sand goes in between my toes and covers my ankles as I stand on the shore concentrating on the point where sea and sky meet. A white sailboat bounces over the waves like soul-light from heaven, where Bunica Anghelina must be sitting in her house of straw sorting out rice. The sea, magnificently strong and mysterious as it is, will calm me, clean my soul, restore my strength, prepare me for another year of hell. Throughout this visit I do little other than memorize images of colors and moods of water. I hoard them and store them like stolen gold coins in my mind.

Amnesty

Sofica, our neighbor who is in her late thirties and single, is called to the Securitate to give information about us. Does she have a choice? We can't tell the difference between her "being interrogated" about us and her being asked to "inform" on us. This is a fine distinction and in any case, however we interpret this, we cannot change our behavior because we pity either her or ourselves. We just avoid talking about "the situation." She makes the trip to the headquarters in Tecuci, she tells the comrades that really there are no American spies coming to the house, and she swears that as far as she can learn from us, there are no collaborators to Dad's crime of protesting against the government. When she returns home it is her and her parents' job to prepare meals for the Securitate comrades who turned the front room of their house into a surveillance residence from which they watch us day and night.

This arrangement strikes me as a chapter from a Kafka novel: it is weirdly comic and unbelievably painful, making Sofica someone who can be trusted by our family and by the police at the same time. She performs her tasks with humor, utmost sincerity, and kindheartedness, her only other job being to feed the horses and look after her parents' garden. She writes to us on bits of paper the questions she is asked and the answers she gives. When there is something she is assigned to ask us, she writes, "They want me to ask you the following," and then intones the question loudly, in the most innocent of voices, content that we are properly warned. We read her notes and then we

burn them. No one shudders any longer at this situation in which the
state police organization has domesticated itself through her, and sits
at the table with us and "smells our farts in the morning," as Bunica
aptly puts it. The rest of the time Sofica tells us wild stories about her
first marriage, her past drinking problems, love affairs. I don't remember any of them. I retreat inward, to her soothing voice crossing days
and nights while I read.

We still hear the night thumps of the Securitate guards changing shifts behind the house. We were ordered to keep the curtains
drawn open, and still comply. People walking on the main street, in
front of the church, can see what we are doing in the kitchen behind
the church. By the same token, we also catch glimpses of the guards
if they jump too close to the window from which light spills over the
fence, toward the altar. *Thump!* Then a hat or a shoulder slides under
the windowsill. We are scared to go out at night. But Sofica has a
special passport into the darkness; she is absolved of fear or at least
of harm when she crosses the murky territories of our front and back
gardens as Dante crossed hell's territory. As she slips in and out of the
various personae carved out for her, I envy her malleability, the way
she keeps herself entertained, the fact that she has a panoramic view of
the government and us. She is a visionary, I tell myself. And we are
lucky to have her around.

I am also impressed with her talent for telling our fortunes in coffee
grounds. Since she is at the house every day and spends many nights
keeping us company while Mom knits, she drinks lots of coffee with
Mom and me, usually seated by the mouth of our wood-burning stove,
where she taps the ashes from her Snagov cigarettes. I get a tin can or
a small pot, boil the water, throw in the coffee, and when the grounds
surface, ready to spill on the stove, I lift it and pour the coffee in cups
without straining it. Once we've finished drinking (and we are supposed to think about our lives when we sip), the fun begins. Sofica
turns each cup upside down on a plate with a circular motion meant
to coat the inside with the soaked grounds. We wait awhile for the

cups to settle and nearly dry, then she turns them right side up, one at a time, the porcelain inside crisscrossed with portents.

"Oh, there is a bear in here, right by the handle, near the rim." Usually that means Mom will be called by the Securitate man for an interrogation.

"Ah, Carmen, I see the bottom of the cup is really black—your soul must be so sad, you're in trouble. Why don't you put the thumb of your right hand straight in the middle of the bottom to see what's the matter?"

And on it goes: flower shapes, particularly roses, are good news; the little lines the coffee makes as it spills toward the edge of the cup are roads, meaning we are to take trips here and there; white at the bottom of the cup means the soul is becoming lighter, more joyful. I am paying lots of attention to her fortune-telling, not only because it seems to me that she prepares Mom for her next encounter with the Securitate, but also because she makes me feel more hopeful about life in general when I am down: every time I am really down, and I am down almost all the time these days, there is the imminent expectation of good news that will come "in the next few days," so I am learning to take the kindness of strangers in the yogurt lines at five in the morning as a good omen or as the "lightness of being" that Sofica promises in coffee fortunes.

If Mom can afford to send me to summer camp or on an excursion to the painted monasteries (where I invariably try to meet all the nuns and give them all the money I have so that they will pray for our souls for as long as my money will pay for), then Sofica reads my fortune as a "long winding road up mountain paths" so that I expect Mom has a surprise up her sleeve for me. I relish Mom's sense of surprising us with odd tickets for excursions, however schoolish and bookish they are, for many times on these trips I fantasize about living in a monastery curled up on a clay or stone windowsill reading books, praying early in the morning to the sound of ancient bells, and helping make haystacks.

Mom, Loredana, Bunica, Cătălin, and I are all addicted to Sofica, partly because she is the only one who comes to visit often and without restrictions (as opposed to most of our relatives and other friends, who are intimidated), and partly because we are all convinced that a woman like her, with the right chances in life, would have been either a gifted psychologist or a truly unforgettable actress, breathing real life into plays. I can envision her insanely skinny body wrapped in light blue jeans and her white T-shirts on the stage, her face changing with her ever-changing hair colors, in and out of the spotlight, thin red lips uttering truths about humanity. She can understand us, I think. She can understand me as I live between silences and words with double meanings, clearly confused about the importance of survival versus the importance of throwing life away, and screaming against this surveillance from the Securitate the way my father exploded against the government. I am positively in love with her and I do my best to serenade her with my guitar and invite her to the Sunday colloquia I started with some high school friends, who aren't too harshly punished by the Securitate for coming to the house.

I also introduce her to my literature teacher, Lucia, who takes risks in coming to see me. Lucia was also asked to inform but she very loudly denied "the offer," telling us about it with a big voice in the house, so the Securitate will register her with their microphones and not bother her again. My thought is that she was spared the punishment that comes with the "refusal" only because she doesn't live right next door like Sofica does. I love Lucia just as intensely, but for different reasons. I love her because I feel sorry for her own suffering— the "vicissitudes" of her life, as we both call them. Her husband comes home from his lover, with whom he now has a baby, only to beat her and to take the money she earns from teaching. He is an abusive alcoholic. She shows me her legs puckered with holes from the forks with which he stabs her. We cry together and I have the key to her flat, where I can go and sleep without microphones listening to my breathing or my waking nightmares. And we read poetry together aloud in her living room, which is always about to be painted; our voices bounce free over the upturned or covered furniture, dirty dishes, piles of clothes and books on the floor, teacups, opened notebooks in which neither she nor I make notes for school.

*

Years slip into one another as we find ourselves again eating the peaches from the tree I planted with my father back in 1980. In 1988 I graduate from high school, passing my baccalaureate with grades that don't inspire Mom to bring me flowers or bake me a cake but that please me given that I wasn't even considered for a fair examination to begin with. Mom knows this too, but there is still in her the pre-prison pride that makes her want my sister and me to earn only top grades. But since my own pride is hurt, there isn't a need to remind her of the humiliations I faced from teachers who asked me questions from parts of the textbooks we hadn't been studying or, conversely, to tell her about the chemistry teacher who, because he likes me (or feels sympathy for me), let me sit in his office listening to flute concertos by Vivaldi under the pretext that I was doing extra or remedial studying.

Things have relaxed considerably since my parents' divorce. Loredana and Cătălin were allowed back in school and Loredana even managed to obtain a place at the coveted teaching lyceum, where she stayed for a year before transferring to a professional school she likes better. But other than school and Mom now being allowed to work at the knitting factory, which is much better than the willow basket factory, not much else has changed.

Except the peaches, which grow outside my window, big, juicy, orange-red flesh bursting from between the leaves as if to declare to the whole insane, punishing world, "Look how beautiful I am. I can break your heart just with the glow of my skin." Every year they come out I think to myself, "Nothing can stifle the will to live. No amount of suffering will stop a peach from growing, just as nothing, no hunger or punishment, will stop a child from smiling." Dad's postcards from prison have continued to arrive sometime in the spring, and we have continued to visit him in August. Each birthday and holiday we cry and wonder when he will come home. And I am pretty much finishing the books Mariana has in her closet, living somewhere between places with foreign names and Sofica's fortunes in coffee grounds.

*

Then one day the TV news at seven o'clock makes Mom faint first, makes me faint second, and brings Sofica screaming from across the street, only to dump cold water on Mom and me: "You two, this is certainly *not* the time to die."

The speaker says, "Comrade Nicolae Ceauşescu announced today that everyone serving ten or more years of prison sentences, except those who committed murders, will be released from penitentiaries across the country. It was decided that since the prisons are overcrowded, a general amnesty is warranted."

Nothing of course is said about political dissidents, or about Amnesty International campaigning for my father, making him "the prisoner of the month" in 1986, or about *Index on Censorship* listing my father with the other East European dissidents, or about Austrian newspapers writing articles about him, or about Radio Free Europe demanding his release.

I feel half-understood shock that my dad might be coming home. Some days I feel my heart beating too fast; it wants to get out of my body and run all by itself up dusty roads, all happy and free. I am giddy. And then I hear myself saying: "He can't come home. It can't be true." The Securitate around the house, our walls with ears in them, this is all a reality, which makes me doubt what I saw on TV.

*

The last time we visited Dad in Aiud, I convinced my mother to take Loredana, me, and some of my friends to cross the Carpathians. We bought train tickets that allowed us to stop and go along the route. The circuit started in Tecuci, crossed the mountains into Transylvania from northern Moldavia, culminated with the prison visit, and ended via the Olt River into the south of the country, then back up through Vrancea. Our backpacking gear was so basic, it included really heavy pots and pans. We packed fresh food—potatoes, tomatoes, onions— half of which we had to throw into the ravines because it rotted during the journey. We were caught in bear territory, rainstorms, blinding fog, and our maps were so bad that we relied on the sound of sheep bells to guide us out of forests. Of course we had an informer with us, a "friend" certainly, but that hardly mattered.

What mattered were the honey groves nestled in high meadows, the white and red polka dot mushrooms dotting the soil beneath trees like dabs of paint in fairy-tale books, the moon hanging like a gypsy coin over precipices, the smell of virgin pine forests cleaning every thought away from my mind. This was the trip in which I fell deeply in love with the soil, the texture, the rivers and springs of my country, the water song over granite, and with the flower called forget-me-not, which will remain hidden, trembling by roadsides, in my heart. There were times when I lay in bright-yellow meadows wanting to bury myself in the swaying flowers, and I burned images into my mind, greedily, happy that my flesh and soul had come out of this earth and no other.

Now, as I flip through my botany textbook thinking of this, I wonder if Dad really will return home and if we can repeat the trip as a complete family, not with friends but just the five of us. When we told him about the trip at a prison visit, his eyes first lit with the images we tried to bring to his mind and then fell into heavy clouds. I think we harmed him by telling him of such free and beautiful things as mountains and rivers. He knows the country, he loves the land, he crisscrossed the mountains many times in many directions, he has the soul of one who hungers for the beautiful things of the earth. Often he told us about a job he had in the western Carpathians, showing movies at village cinemas. Dad would drive the reels from one village to another up the narrow roads and passes and announce from his van speakers the name of the movie and the time as he went through the main streets. People loved him, hosted him for the night, and gave him lots of wine. He said that he had seen much of the country in this way, that the country was stunningly beautiful.

Often I wonder what would have happened if Dad had never returned to Moldavia, hadn't met and married Mom. I would have missed so many stories if I wasn't his child. As it was, my parents met by accident. Dad was driving through Drăgănești when a car accident happened just in front of my grandparents' house. He stopped to help and Mom also rushed out to help. Dad noticed her by the well. When Bunica Anghelina saw them speaking with each other, she invited Dad inside to freshen up and have something to drink. She told Mom, "That's the son-in-law I want: smart, well-built, and good-looking," and with these words she broke Mom's heart because she was already courted by someone else. A few days later Dad returned to ask Mom out for a movie. On the way there he wanted to be friends with her; at the movie theater he asked her to be forever best friends; and when he brought her home he kissed her and proposed marriage. Thus Dad was welcomed into the family. My parents experienced love at first sight. I can't imagine all of us being back together again—it would be too much happiness. I wonder if the announcement about the amnesty isn't something that Mom, Sofica, and I invented.

*

It's getting dark outside and I am not studying. Everyone, including Bunica, is away. The phone rings.

"*Alo*, is this Carmen?"

"Yes, and may I ask who is calling?"

"Do you not recognize me?"

"No. Is there something you want?"

"Carmen, it's your dad. I am coming home."

Shocked into the thought that this might be a Securitate officer playing games with me to see what I might say or do, I say curtly, "My father is in prison and maybe you should mind your own business."

"Carmenuțo, you don't recognize your father? I just got off the train. I am on my way to see your uncle and aunt. Where is your mom?"

His voice comes back to me not from a place of forgetting but from disbelief to belief. And yet the happiness does not come to me yet, guarded as I am from the habit of controlling myself in the earshot of microphones.

"Dad, Mom is at work. Take Tanti Balașa and she will walk you there. Bunica and Cătălin are on their way home, and when you get here I will be waiting for you. Loredana is away at school."

We both hang up at the same time. I am surely dreaming.

When my father walks through the door holding Mom's hand, Cătălin and Bunica are already here.

"My son, I lived to see you again," says Bunica through her tears.

"Dad, there are microphones everywhere, so don't talk about anything important," I write to him.

In the empty place the necessary silence carves into the room, everyone cries, and Cătălin, in the arms of my father, unfamiliar to him other than by name and prison visits, asks him, "Why don't you have any hair on your head?"

We all go to sleep in the same bed in our street clothes, Bunica, Dad, Mom, Cătălin, and me, and I swear I can smell the Aiud chains on the jacket of his black suit piled on the chair.

House Arrest

Our hallway is filled with boots and shoes of all sizes; the hangers groan under winter clothes. Tanti Săftica arrived around eleven in the morning with a hen and fresh eggs in a wicker basket. This morning she wears her scarf with pink roses, the pistils sewn with tiny gold threads. Her usual worried look is suppressed and when I kiss her cheeks she smells like the fresh wind outside. Bunicu, blue eyes moist, walnut oil in his hair, and his black church suit freshly dusted, still smelling of incense, carries a few bottles of red wine that clink against each other in a stained canvas bag. Titi and Ionica, Fănel, Costel and Nuța, Florin—Tanti Săftica's sons and their families—have brought red carnations, feta cheese, sour cream, and upside-down cheese pies. Tanti Balașa and Uncle Dan come with freshly made meatballs and stuffed grape leaves, still warm in deep bowls. All the women are crowded in the summer kitchen preparing lunch. The men are divided between splitting wood to keep the fire in the winter kitchen going for baking bread and drinking the first glasses of wine. Loredana is away at school but we called this morning and we're expecting her to come on the first train. Cătălin and I just walk around listening in to various conversations and trying to calm Bunica Floarea, who is so excited that she wants to tell everyone how much pain and suffering her darling son has caused her and how from now on she is going to make sure to beat him up and keep him close to her skirts "like a good mother does."

As much as the occasion is Dad's return home, everyone congratulates Mom. "See, now you have your husband back so there should be no more worrying for you," says Tanti Balaşa, who truly has been a wise and patient older sister to Mom in Dad's absence.

"A woman without a husband is much weaker, so now that you are a full family again, make sure to keep him out of trouble, this husband of yours," smiles Tanti Săftica, who is the one who pretty much saw that we survived day to day.

Mom glows between her two sisters, her thin cheeks now the color of Cameo apples, hands deep in dough, forearms white as the dough. I almost don't believe that she dug out her knitted purple mohair dress and curled her hair; I must have been still asleep! Uncle Dan pats her on the shoulder and says, "There you are, so proud with your husband home now, you hearty little thing. See, you and the children survived, and now we don't have to worry about you anymore. And look how your little Cătălin is growing!"

Actually, I think, this should be a meal in which we celebrate our relatives, because only they know the interrogations, intimidations, and threats they received from the Securitate over the past five years just because they came to visit us and support us.

The conversation we are not having is precisely this: How did each of them find out about Dad's demonstration and arrest, what questions were they asked at the interrogations, how did they cope with being followed and summoned to give "reports" of their "activities" at random times during most weeks and months for all these years? Questions such as these never arise, and in the placid face of Bunicu, Uncle Dan, and Cousin Titi, each smiling, content to sit at the table with Dad and look into his eyes, still red from the train journey, in the perfection of their starched shirts and ties, no one would guess they have been suffering just because they are related to him.

As for Dad, I am dying to hear the exact sensation he felt when he was told that he was free. I can only imagine the first full breath of cold winter air outside the Aiud walls, the trepidation of the shocked chest.

Only much later in life, away from the microphone's reach, will I find out that he was put in the same cell (number 20) in Aiud in which he was given solitary confinement some twenty years before, and that the guard, the same man who watched him in his youth, recognized him. He will tell me, when I mention to him that I happened to walk around Sligo, Ireland, one day and maybe through a fault in memory the city walls struck me a lot like the city walls of Aiud, that the night he was freed from prison he thought they were tricking him, sending him outside the gates only to murder him, and when he boarded the train with his bundle of clothes, he thought he was dreaming. All the way home, two days on trains, he thought he was dreaming, and he loved the smell of free people and cold fresh air coming through the doors at the stations. When I will turn twenty-six years old, on my birthday, he will tell me, lips red from dark merlot and hands busy with a piece of cheese, that when he was twenty-six he was already a political dissident suffering his first beatings.

"Oh, Carmenuţo, they turned me into a sandbag, handcuffed and blindfolded me, took me through a labyrinth of corridors in a musty-smelling basement, and they passed me from one to another using their feet to kick and their fists to smash my cheeks. But I fought so that words can be free to be uttered and heard."

Never mind what I will feel like hearing this story.

And there are other questions that have been turning in my mind for years: Did my father ever feel guilty for leaving me in the house with no food and no indication of when he would return? Did he miss me? Did he ever feel sorry for leaving Cătălin ill and Mom helpless in the hospital? Did he regret not saying goodbye to Loredana, or did he ever think about her? Did he think what might happen to us because of him? Did he really think that we, his flesh and blood, were expendable in comparison with fighting for human rights for the whole country? Of course, I cannot ask these questions on the night of his release, but when I eventually do, he will say he thought about it and sometimes it takes sacrificing a family for a country. Never mind how

I will feel *then*. It is better not to judge; it is better to try to understand, to observe. Judgment can be dangerous in situations such as these. And my question is too long anyway.

Now Titi, his black curls falling on his forehead, is busy explaining to Dad that he just started to build a gladiola farm in Bunicu's backyard, and he found bulbs that will put forth flowers of all colors. "I am building a glasshouse for them, too, and I want to sell them at the market. It's good business with all the weddings in the summer, and it brings extra money. My little daughters can sell them and I will help them on the weekends."

So the conversation in the earshot of the microphones is about aging dogs, cats going blind, gardens, growing children. In a normal situation, no one would imagine that there would be anything else worth discussing over a long Sunday lunch in celebration of someone's return home. But then again, how many people return from prison on any given day? The aromas of the food, the warm fire, the tune of conversations filling the whole house, and the first blushes in the cheeks from the wine make my heart glad. I take a big glass of wine myself and walk around drinking from it with Cătălin perched like a rucksack on my back, himself eating a piece of cake, the crumbs falling in my hair. The red carnations in the white glass vase on the table seem to gather all of our feelings inside their petals. We celebrate everything with carnations.

"Miorița, we're going to the village hall to get remarried," I hear Dad say to Mom.

"Of course, we'll go first thing in the morning. We will take my father for a witness."

*

Even though she has been barking at Securitate men for five years, Bombonica never tires of the opportunity to aim for the trouser legs or the hems of their coats and bare her teeth in the most expressive show of displeasure. I absolutely love her for it and now, in the first days since Dad arrived home, she gets lots of praise from him too. The man this morning, with his black city hat and his brown leather coat extending below his knees, a rectangular stiff leather case in his hand, wants to speak with my father alone. But the doors are left open and we do not quiet Bombonica until he begs us to, and I listen to what he says from across the hall.

"I am here to inform you that you are under house arrest. This means that we want you to report to the police station each morning and each evening and that you are allowed to go only to the local shop next door for your food. If you want to visit relatives and friends, you must first inform us of the purpose and length of your visit, tell us who you will be visiting, and report to the station on your way out and on the way back. My suggestion is that you go absolutely nowhere in order to avoid complications. We are watching you from across the street, behind the house, the house at the corner of the street, and will interview everyone who comes to visit you here. Day and night we will be around the house, so if you attempt to outsmart us, know that we will put you back in jail. Is this perfectly clear to you?"

"Yes."

"Good. Your wife and children are permitted to go to school, work, and do shopping, but no one is permitted to leave the perimeter of Tecuci. No one in the family is to travel any farther than to this village and the town."

"Dad, how long is this going to last?" I barge in right as the Securitate man is leaving.

"Leave me alone!"

*

We are asleep. The oil candle on the eastern wall, above the stove, has gone out. I don't know if I am dreaming, but Dad shouts incomprehensible words about a thief while Mom is trying to hold him. They are near the door. Dad is holding on to the hatchet.

"There is no one, Nelu. I can't hear anything in the house."

"Are you certain of it? Let's go together and check all the rooms and all the closets. No one comes into my house, no one or I will kill him!"

"He is having nightmares," Bunica Floarea says. "A while ago he was begging to be given a break from something. I am not sure how your poor mother will deal with him after I leave in the morning. I told him many times, you don't play with these people, you will be messed up for good. Now look what's become of your father. Go back to sleep, children."

*

When I come home from school I find Dad in the living room rummaging through the cupboards, all the papers, Mom's scarves, my books and journals on the floor.

"What are you looking for?"

"Leave me alone. I am looking to see if everything is how I left it."

"Dad, minus the whole-house search in which everything got messed up and your audiotapes, papers, gloves, and typewriters were confiscated by the comrades, everything is here, yes, though probably in the order Loredana and I managed to put it in when we reassembled the house. What is your problem?"

He looks at me in amazement and I keep going, now angry. "Are you afraid we erased the traces of you? No one forgot about you, no one emptied your closets and gave your clothes to the Gypsies, don't worry. I have been wearing your green pajamas if you don't terribly mind, since they are warmer and bigger than mine, but you shouldn't protest about that. I am not going to put away everything you have been taking out. *You* put everything back!"

I run into the kitchen and throw my backpack on the table. Dad is very weird in more than one way. When he is hungry, he asks permission to eat from whoever is around. When he goes to the bathroom, he asks permission. When he wants another glass of water, he asks permission to drink. Our faces are raw from crying because we don't know what to do with him.

"Of course you can do anything," Mom says. "It's your house, remember?"

But he has had the same red eyes and the same tortured expression on his face since he returned. He doesn't smile (not that he often did before). The house arrest is getting to him. Like a bear kept in a cage, he paces around the house, now intimidated, now angry, now afraid that we no longer care for him, now feeling useless, now feeling as if he no longer has pride. Little by little this house has slipped out of our ownership; it feels more like a place where we are all trapped. His trips to the police station are making him even more tense, and his destroying the house like this drives me insane.

Today even the village policeman complained that he has lost weight and is tired of jumping the fence and watching us night after night, with Bombonica aiming for his legs as if she had never smelled him before. He didn't notice that Bombonica also just gave birth so she is even more agitated than usual with people coming into our yard and behind the house all the time. He is focused on complaining to Dad.

"You must understand, I have also got a family and before you threw yourself into this shit I was having a peaceful life in this village, with food on the table and no one coming to inspect me. Now they torture me because you escaped my attention and did your unthinkable act in Bucureşti. They practically live in my house, breathing down my neck. Everyone got in trouble and hates you, from the town Securitate boss to the district boss. I am not sure when this will end, but you surely destroyed my life too."

*

The trains still get stranded on the line and the five in-the-morning bus from Drăgăneşti to Tecuci sometimes still gets stuck in the snow. When I come home one day with the two jars of yogurt and the loaf of bread, Mom and Dad are in the living room with another Securitate man. I give him as ugly a look as I can, but when I turn to go into the kitchen I hear the words "social parasitism," so I return to the living room and sit down, staring at him while he continues to speak as if I had not entered the room.

"So, as I said, you must get a job very soon or else you will be put in prison for social parasitism. Just make sure to report to the station before and after work. Any deviation from this, you already know what we will do. Goodbye for now."

Mom talks with Tanti Balaşa, who gets Dad a job at the factory where she works as a chef, serving lunch. Two days after Dad starts, though, a car aims straight for him as he crosses the parking lot to go to lunch. When Dad reports this to the police he is accused of not wanting to work, of exaggerating an accident. "It happens to everyone, losing concentration while they are getting out of the parking lot," the policeman says.

Somehow I envy Loredana, who went back to school after she came to welcome Dad home. She isn't around him and his problems as much as I am. But since the phone is tapped, and I am not allowed to go and see her and she is not allowed to come home other than for spring vacation, there is no way I can tell her what is going on and how impossible our lives have become. Each day there is the added game of waiting to see if Dad returns home from work in one piece or if he goes mad again. This is intolerable. Mom has become so tense with Dad's rummaging through the house and his nightmares that today she smashed the clothing iron on the floor as he walked in asking yet another nonsensical question about something, I don't even know what, he found in one of the cupboards. Mom never loses her temper, so as the hot iron burned a mark into the rug I understood that she has come to the end of her patience. Cătălin began crying and I covered his mouth with my palm while I ran outside with him, into the destroyed day.

I take Dad for a little walk to the end of our street and say to him, very quietly, that he doesn't have the slightest clue what we have been living through, how the Securitate have keys to the house and the car incident is something I am used to because it happens to *me* at least once a week. I also explain to him that he needs to see the reality of an abandoned family to which he returned not with roses but with more trouble than before he left. He doesn't understand. I can see from the bemused look on his face that he thinks I am still twelve years old, not seventeen, Loredana is still eleven, not sixteen, and Cătălin is still a baby swaddled in blankets, not five years old. He doesn't understand what it was like for us to grow up without a father, having to fend for ourselves at a time when most children have their fathers to provide for them and teach them things. I return weary from my attempted conversation with him.

"This is the freedom you left us with when you left, just like the freedom you now experience," I say through tight jaws.

"Carmen, your mind is limited, your mind is domestic. You must be a visionary and you must sacrifice for your vision!"

"I never wanted to be part of your vision. You never asked any of us to be part of your vision. You just took our support without even as much as a word of thanks. Remember you told me I will eat even fire? Well, I did, and I don't thank you for it. You are lucky we have microphones in the house and I cannot explain so many things I am dying to explain to you about your vision and my life!"

I want to lecture him, to preach to him, to change his life, but I also see the futility. Change his life into *what*, exactly, when we are all being kept like animals in the cage of the house we built with dreams of long years of happiness? I feel guilty too. Just as he doesn't know what we experienced in our supposed freedom, I don't know what he experienced in his captivity. Adding to this psychological suffocation is the fact that we do not have a physical space in which to speak, to argue, to debate, to win each other over, or just to explain ourselves. We do not even trust that the fences on the street have no ears.

My Visit
to the American Embassy

Bombonica's pups squeal like out-of-tune violins. They suck at her teats until she gets tired and starts walking around the garden with them still stuck to her. We feed her and pet her to make sure she stays put so the pups don't go hungry. They all seem to look like her, whitish and soft. She is more nervous around strangers now, more protective. To my undisguised pleasure, the Securitate must take the brunt of it. I am thinking that soon we'll have an army of dogs to bark at them till they turn deaf.

*

It fell to Dad to find out early this morning that our Bombonica was poisoned overnight. He found her in Mom's garden with her head aimed at the front door as if to say that she loved us. When he called us outside, there was foam spilled from her mouth all over the ground and she was motionless. The pups were sucking at her dead teats making pitiful sounds. I remember Dad coming home with Bombonica under his coat when she was still a puppy, how he was so excited he didn't even realize he was screaming at me and Loredana not to fight with each other over her and not to smother her with hugs and kisses. I feel sorry that Dad had to be the one to find her dead. I know how much he loves animals. He taught us to waltz with Bursucu to the tune of "The Blue Danube" before he brought us Bombonica. Loredana and I took turns dancing with him on the porch, his paws on our shoulders, the waltz coming from the tape player and all kinds of "up, doggy, here, come up" from us, while Mom looked in dismay at the dirt streaks the dog left on our clothes. At Iveşti Dad had Leo always following him around the store.

For me, the death of Bombonica, who was clearly poisoned by the Securitate, means a lot more than reflecting about Dad's loss. This dog was, until this morning, the outward expression of how I have felt since I was ten years old. And she has given voice to everything I have felt toward the Securitate since they came into our house and took our family portraits off the walls.

"Let's look after the pups the best we can until we find them safer homes, so they don't have the same fate as their mother."

"Okay, Dad."

*

Days and nights are eerily silent without Bombonica. The Securitate men come to ask their questions without being disturbed and often we are surprised by knocking on the door or by the sound of them clearing their throats before they call for Dad. Now the thumps behind the house at night come alone, punctuated only by the eleven o'clock shift change. Loredana is still away at school but we have called Bunica Floarea to stay with us so she can look after Cătălin while Mom, Dad, and I disperse for work and school and meet at home in the evenings.

*

Through a complicated chain of events that culminated during the past year, I fell in love with Sorin, who is in my year of high school and, like me, is preparing for the university entrance examination. We met in our veterinary medicine program shortly before my father came home from prison, but it is only recently that we fell in love. He began by bringing me small bouquets of flowers, snowdrops or lilies of the valley, and leaving them inside my desk, between books. After school he walks with me to the bus station through the botanic gardens and sometimes he carries me in his arms over the bridge, reciting poetry to me. We both like Nichita Stănescu and Ana Blandiana but always go back to Eminescu or Coşbuc. We are both fatalistic, we believe that love is to be declared and never spent; we don't believe in happiness, we believe in the reality of yearning and suffering. Sometimes I am so tired from all the work I do around the house and all the early-morning yogurt and bread lines, I fall asleep in his arms.

"Do you know that you snore really loud, and we are only sitting on the bench? Do you never sleep?"

Our romance is just this, since I am followed everywhere and we cannot go to movies or indulge in long afternoons of walking around lazily, holding hands. One day at the station, as everyone is busy cramming into the bus, he bows toward my lips in a slightly confusing gesture of giving me my backpack, which he carries. Just as his lips nearly touch mine and I think I am going to pass out from expectation, Dad's voice comes from the bus louder and clearer than anything I have ever heard: "Carmenuţo, are you coming home with this bus?"

Sorin and I turn bright red, and that is how my family knows that I am in love. He rushes with me to the bus door, introduces himself, and waits for Dad to extend his hand.

"He is a very nice boy, Carmenuţo."

"Yep, Dad, I know, I know. Why on earth are you on this bus anyway? Aren't you supposed to be at work?"

"I went to Bucureşti to meet two friends. I will tell you later. Looks like everyone here got in trouble because I escaped the house arrest for the day, so I must stop at the police station on the way back. You go on straight home."

*

It's past two in the morning. The oil candle below the icon has finished burning and the face of Saint Mary with her child has disappeared into the darkness. We are woken by the ringing of the telephone. When Dad picks up, the man on the other end yells loud enough that the rest of us can hear "You fucking criminal, I am going to kill you and throw you into a ditch. Bugan, you hear me, I will cut you into pieces, you shit."

Then the line goes dead. We cannot talk because of the microphones, but I hear my heart pounding so loud with fear and anger that I can feel it push against my ribs. From now on this becomes a routine two-in-the-morning call that Dad doesn't answer. So many of these episodes will never be discussed by my family. No one will ever know how each of us internalized those brutal words coming into our house, into our sleep.

In the morning, after we wake up, Dad writes on a piece of paper, "I think we should consider asking for political asylum at some embassy and leave the country. I have a feeling they want us out. There is nothing here we are allowed to do and it doesn't look like they will let us live, either."

We pass the note around, Mom and I, and each of us responds in writing.

"I think it's a bad idea. They will probably kill you because now they will think you want to go to some foreign country and expose the government. Plus, I don't want to leave my family, and we have three children. Where will we go?"

"Dad, I want to apply to the university to get a degree in biology in Iaşi. I want to go there. I don't think it's a good idea."

"Mioara, I will come to pick you up from work this afternoon so we can take a short walk in town before we come home. We need to talk about this. It is the only option I see."

"Okay."

None of us touches the bread or the jar of plum jam, the kitchen smells almost nostalgically of our linden tea. I secretly do not want to leave Sorin. I have fantasies about our being university students together in Iaşi, walking around the hilly streets and holding hands in medieval churches, having rose-flavored ice cream in the parks and kissing at midday in cafés with no Securitate following me. And I would like to go dancing with him. I would like us to go to museums and imagine what it would have been like if we had been born during the Renaissance somewhere far from here. I cannot see myself saying goodbye to him, and now I try to push the image of his face out of my mind's eye.

In the evening Mom looks tense and Dad looks determined. He drafts a letter to the Internal Ministry headquarters in București asking that our immediate family be allowed to emigrate. He decides to post the letter in the morning. Dad has a point. We are prisoners in the house we built for ourselves and no one knows how long we will be able to live with these threats on the phone, with cars attempting to run us over, with house arrest. It doesn't feel like anything belongs to us any longer, even our relatives. Sofica and Lucia have stopped coming around. Everyone is being harassed. Sorin's sister prohibited him from walking me to the bus station because my family has "problems," so I assume she was also harassed. Only Sorin doesn't stop seeing me, and neither does my best friend, Aurora, who has been around the house nearly every day and is so close to me, I never even think of her—she has become an extra sister in a way. No one bothers her about coming to see me, I have no idea why, and without her it would be hard to get up in the mornings. When we go to her house we can talk freely until our cheeks and jaws hurt.

*

We're watching the evening news before the lights go out. Without Bombonica barking, we now have less warning, so sometimes we are taken by surprise by shadows under the windowsill. Tonight the announcer says something about the rise of inflation; we are crowding in front of the TV to see the new higher prices for food. Suddenly the whole TV moves!

"Well, that's strange," says Mom. "It's like a ghost just pushed it."

As Dad attempts to slide the TV back into place, the cable is pulled from it so violently that his arms are jolted. We see the cable being yanked outside through its hole in the windowsill and almost simultaneously duck on the floor out of some kind of instinct. We realize that the Securitate man outside is pulling the television cable to freak us out or annoy us, but in this moment of shock I am not sure what *else* will happen. With the curtain open there is no shelter from their view other than the floor. All of us breathe heavily, then slowly crowd on the same bed, under the blankets. The lights go off all over the village a while later, making us at least feel safer under the blindness of darkness. I make up my mind tonight to agree with my father about leaving the country.

*

Early in the morning, Mom, Dad, and I are back at the table with our linden tea, untouched bread, and the unopened jar of jam. Dad scribbles on my pad, "One of us must go to the American Embassy and ask for political asylum. I have the phone number for someone there from my friends; they will know about our situation but will need paperwork and testimony."

"Nelu, you can't go with this surveillance."

"They said they are not responsible for what might happen to me if I ever break the curfew again."

"Mom, you can't go either because you too have house arrest. I will go. I want to go."

"No, we are not risking *you*, Carmen. One of us might go."

"But it's easier for me to sneak out at night. Why don't we check the night trains?"

"Mioara, I trust Carmen, she should go. Carmen, you say you are going to Bucureşti to renew your prescription for glasses. I will give you the phone numbers of my friends Iancu and Drăghici. You stay with Iancu, and Drăghici will meet you to give you the phone number of the American Embassy. Once you're in the embassy, you will be safe, no matter what the Securitate say they will do to you. Here are the phone numbers you need. You call these men from the station."

"Okay, Mom, Dad, I'll do it, don't worry, you'll see. I read lots of detective novels!"

I spend the rest of the day mortified and excited, excited because I get to do something useful, to try something. I am happy for not being so important to the Securitate that I might escape their attention. I am also proud that I am the only one who can provide hope for our family, so all day long I make sure to settle myself, to bring myself to a calm, even keel, so that my parents can entrust me with this second adult errand of my life.

In the evening Dad gives me the train schedule: 2:30 a.m. from Drăgănești to Tecuci, 3:00 a.m. the fast train from the Tecuci main station. Mom sews Dad's paperwork—the document which attests that Dad was condemned for propaganda against the socialist regime, and the exit document from Aiud—into the lining of my coat. The rest, the testimony, I will have to write for myself once I am inside the embassy. And if I am stopped on the way there, I am to insist that I am changing my glasses prescription, also insisting that since no one required me to report to the police station every day I assumed it would be okay to see an optometrist.

*

Even the air is asleep at two in the morning. Usually it gets colder in the evening, everything falls into inertia overnight, and I feel the coolness return at around five on my way to the yogurt lines. Now the air is still, almost breathless. I slip out of the house in the darkness and leave without closing the gate, so as not to make any noise. My heart is pounding so quickly and my temples are pounding so hard from tension and fear, the only way to steady myself is to jog all the way to the train station. "Take the back way by the woods," Dad whispered, "and stay hidden behind the pillars at the stations in order to be as unobservable as possible."

I have no trouble getting to București. Mr. Iancu collects me and shows me where he and his family live so I know where to go back to rest before the journey home.

Mr. Drăghici meets me at Hanul lui Manuc, helps me memorize

the telephone number of the American Embassy and a statement in English: "My name is Carmen Bugan. I would like someone please to come outside the gates to collect me. I am expected."

Then he gives me directions to the metro station nearest the embassy and tells me that from there it will be exactly a two-minute walk to the gates; whatever happens, I have to walk through the patrols and *not* stop until I get to the gate, even if the guards yell at me not to cross the street and not to go near the embassy. I go into the subway and exit at my station so fast that people and images scroll and zoom in front of me too quickly for me to feel anything.

When I call from the public phone at the subway station I am told an official will be outside immediately. At the corner of the street where I am to turn, a uniformed soldier yells at me that this is a restricted area, I must turn around. As he speaks, a young woman in a bright blue skirt and a white shirt comes out of the gates, sees me, and comes straight for me. She grabs my hand, and I feel that she has a cool, thin *American* hand, much softer than mine. We walk among the guards together into the embassy and she addresses me in Romanian, telling me that I am safe now. She asks how she may help me. After I give her my name, she confirms that they were expecting someone from our family. They are familiar with our case, so I should just wait a minute while she arranges an interview with me.

All I see is a writing pad and a pen in front of me.

"Please, if you have your father's prison papers, we would like to see them. We would like to know if you and your family were persecuted for your father's demonstration in 1983. Tell us what happened, tell us everything, write everything in this notebook. How many people would you like to come with you to America other than your immediate family? Please make sure to list them on this form." And she hands me a form too.

"But which part about our persecution would you like to know? Dad is under house arrest and I cannot talk about what happened to him in prison because I don't know. As for our family, where shall I begin? I don't know what is most important to tell you."

"Just relax and write everything you can remember."

Five hours later, suffering from intense thirst, my right wrist hurting, I am finally stopped.

"Your mother was forced to divorce, your siblings were kicked out of school, you are under house arrest, all of you, you receive death threats on the phone in the middle of the night, and there are microphones recording everything you say? I think this is enough. Please tell your family that you will receive political asylum and visas very soon and that we will write to you about having all of you come here to begin filling out the forms necessary for emigration."

"Can I stay here until you call them? I am scared to go outside now. Maybe they will kill me on the train home because I came here."

"We already called the Internal Ministry and told them that you intend to emigrate. You are now under international protection. They might harass you, but there is nothing they can do to actually harm you. You cannot stay here, so you must go."

The nice woman walks me back outside the gates. When we shake hands, I look for the first time at her very blond hair falling gently on her thin face, at her very light blue eyes. She is stunningly beautiful and I am certain I am confusing her with an angel.

*

As soon as I turn the corner from the American Embassy, I see a guard coming toward me.

"You whore, what the fuck were you doing in the embassy?"

He hits me in the chest with his automatic weapon, lengthways. For the first time in my life I have a gun crossing my chest.

"Bitch! You come with me now."

He pushes me into the observation booth at the corner where another man insults me and asks for a "written declaration" about my audience.

"The official told me that she called the Securitate headquarters already and you are not going to touch me because I am under international protection. I am not going to give you a written declaration."

I muster every bit of courage I can. I maintain my calm and play the role of someone who cannot possibly be intimidated.

After about forty-five minutes someone else arrives, someone in charge. He asks me, without introducing himself, the purpose of my visit to the embassy.

"My family and I are going to emigrate to America."

"Who gave you the number of the embassy and directions here?"

"I was told I should feel free not to give you any details. I am under American protection now with my entire family."

"Go home on the first train and do not come here again."

*

"Success, success!" Mr. Iancu jumps, happy with my audience at the embassy. "Please give your father my greetings and let's take you to the train station now. You must do what they tell you, but don't be afraid."

"And you? What will happen to you and Mr. Drăghici?"

"Well, I was in prison with your father. I know how to deal with them, and they don't know you have seen Drăghici, do they? Plus, you are not obligated to speak with them anymore. Just keep saying you're under protection and hope they will leave you alone."

*

All the way home, hungry and nauseated at the same time, exhausted from lack of sleep and the feel of the gun across my chest, I shiver. The train makes few stops, but at each one I expect someone to come and hurl me out an opened door. I am terrified. Then I realize, as nothing happens with each passing hour, that maybe this is what they wanted us to do, or else something *would* have happened to me. I think they want us out.

I feel homesick, homesick for the way the sun pounces over Sorin's dark curls, which in turn bounce over his forehead, playing hide-and-seek with his tar-black eyes; homesick for my *bunicu* with his Steluţa and his cart, his hat over his white hair smelling of hay; homesick for Bunica Anghelina and her story about the cuckoo bird from Lugoj. I feel as if I am drifting up toward the ceiling of the train, weightless from the adrenaline of the first thoughts that I might, after all, leave everything behind. I miss Loredana immensely. I want to tell her about my adventure, my arrest, the gun, that we may be going to a place called America.

When I was in second grade I became fascinated with a French lesson about traveling. In the textbook there was a drawing of a man wearing a long spring coat like my father's; he was standing in line at the airport, holding on to a suitcase. The text under the photo said "Bon voyage." I remember puzzling over the idea of traveling outside my country, the sheer excitement of it, the excitement of returning home from another country. Now this image is playing in my head. I am not entirely certain what "exile" really is; it still seems as distant in time and as nostalgic as Ovid's *Tristia* on our Black Sea. I want to talk with Loredana about this so much I hurt.

When I stumble in the door, late in the evening, I write to my parents, "I did it. They will contact us now. I gave the papers and the testimony. They said we will all go to America." Dad takes me in his arms and kisses me while Mom holds me as if to double-check that I am still alive.

"Bravo, Carmenuţo," Dad says aloud. "You're your father's daughter." For the first time he is happy, or perhaps for the first time he notices me for something I can offer.

Last Summer
with Bunicu Neculai

Aurora is one of the few friends of my own age I have left, mostly because all the other kids disappeared once the Securitate pretty much
moved into the house. She began coming around more after Mom divorced Dad, when things relaxed slightly. I have called my friendship
with her the sisterhood of lilacs since I was about fifteen, when, one
evening, we brought armfuls of lilacs from my grandfather's garden,
and all the other lilacs bending their branches over the fences around
the village, into our living room. After we placed them in vases all
over the house I put on Vivaldi's *Spring*. I am not sure which I remember most, the music, the music smelling of lilacs, or the stems of the
flowers stained with the blood from our scratched hands. That evening when we crossed the threshold between warm acquaintances and
friends, every street seemed to smell of cool wet lilacs, cats were sitting
on the fences with their tails curled under them, and dogs were barking in the yards. Aurora looked so animated all through our foray for
the flowers that I could guess, in the darkness, the pink in her cheeks.

Today we received our visas from the American Embassy. We must
go to București for the blood tests and paperwork, so I must break the
news to her that I am leaving, never to return. My palms are sweaty.
What I am about to tell her seems so far-fetched, it almost sounds like
a lie. But to tell her this I must face myself what it will be like to have
the rest of my life without a truly close childhood friend around. I
feel the same way about Sorin and about some other friends I made in
high school, book-reading friends, who for a year or so came around

the house on Sundays to talk about novels and poetry, and sometimes to sing. Everything stopped when Dad returned home. Things are complicated now with Sorin too because he is going to begin compulsory army service in just a couple of weeks, so ours will be a double leave-taking. This is what I am thinking about while my father, all excited, reads the letter from the embassy over and over again.

"How are we going to tell the family that we're leaving, Nelu? My father is an old man. With his Alzheimer's, he will not even understand the seriousness of this. Do you realize that we will not be here for his death or for your mother's death? Do you even know where we're going?"

"Grand Rapids, Michigan, it says here, Miorițo. Let's have a look at the map. See, the Great Lakes are there!"

"Mom, we should tell Loredana about this. School is nearly over."

"I think we should get ready for the trip to București now and apply for passports," says Dad, for whom leaving means only an end to suffering. He is clearly the only one who is looking forward to leaving the country; the rest of us have ties with people, with places, even with suffering from the time he was away.

*

Loredana is at home now. We are again together as we were when I was ten years old, only this morning we find ourselves in a waiting room, at the passport office in Galați. This is no longer a trip to eat ice cream while we walk along the Danube, watching the big ships come into the port or whiling away afternoons in gardens filled with summer flowers. I remember spending time in the bookstores with my parents, me looking for poetry and Dad looking for political philosophy while Mom and Loredana flipped through art books.

The man behind the window asks us, "Do you think in America the dogs run around with bagels on their tails? You'll be digging in the dust with the rest of the immigrants building roads and bridges for the fat rich Americans and you'll be scrounging for the cheapest piece of meat you can find at their supermarkets—they'll feed the dogs before they'll feed you. You stupid people! There is no honor in living in another man's backyard."

This man, who probably informs on his own mother, for how else could he work at the passport office, this man serving a government that keeps us in a cage because Dad wanted food and electricity for the whole country, this man throws the typical vile rhetoric of patriotism in our faces when we have no choice but to go. Only a couple of days ago the village policeman told Dad again that they cannot wait for us to leave, for we even ruined the lives of the Securitate! I want to jump over the counter and put my whole fist in this man's mouth. Does he not know that *my* childhood was sacrificed on the altar of love for this country? How empty people become when their stomachs are full.

But we are more worried about paying for our train tickets to Italy, so we make plans for selling our furniture to see how much money we can raise. As for the house, we debate which part of the family to leave it to as a gift. We know, for example, that Tanti Săftica's sons, especially Fănel, who just got married a couple of years ago, could probably make good use of it. Our cursed house.

*

It's eight in the morning and the knock on the door this time is not the Securitate—they are already walking around behind the church and in the blind woman's field next door in full daylight. This man is the village accountant, who demands to speak with both Mom and Dad at the same time. He delivers the news on the doorstep just like this: "We are required to confiscate your house and all of the property left in it. We know you have already sold the biggest pieces of furniture, but now the village council has required me to ask you to evacuate the house in the next forty-eight hours, at which time I will come to collect the keys. I am sorry about this, Mr. Bugan, Mrs. Bugan."

The man clearly is uncomfortable, more so because he was one of my parents' fairly close acquaintances before my father demonstrated. He had been through some serious interrogations because of my father.

"Are you certain of this?" asks Mom in total disbelief.

"Yes. Very well, then, I must leave you. I will be back for the keys."

I can only imagine the shame he feels having to do this to us. He always struck me as a nice man. But I am also angry with him, for, like the others, he became one of the "official" people out of fear or convenience or both. Seeing him, and others like him, often makes me wonder what would happen if I reached an age at which the Securitate forced *me* to become an informer.

*

I am not certain I can feel the hours whirl now. We are all waiting for the village accountant to collect the house keys. No one wants to give them away, so in an act of making the break between myself and the very earth I love, I take charge. "Fine, I will give him the keys."

Suddenly I am back a couple of weeks, in the middle of the night when we sold my bedroom furniture. I took the bedsheets, duvets, and pillows, stripping everything down to the mattress for the last time. The books I had been reading and loving were stored on the headboard shelves—*Tess of the D'Urbervilles, Madame Bovary, Germinal, Nana, King Arthur,* and my favorite childhood book, *Amintiri din Copilărie* (Memories of childhood) by Ion Creangă, a writer who also grew up in Moldavia, and whose stories seemed to complete my own childhood adventures playing by the river and memorizing household superstitions so thoroughly that I cannot distinguish between his life and mine. It is from him that I learned how to bring out the sun from under the clouds: *"Rîzi copile cu părul bălai la soare că poate sar mai indrepta vremea! Si vremea se indrepta după risul meu."* (Little child with blond hair, smile at the sun to bring it out! And the weather would brighten at my laughter.) The winters were always cold, gathering all of us in the winter kitchen, but the springs, summers, and autumns were all mine, in my bedroom. Our peaches grew just outside the windows with their associations, their beautiful sorrows. A book with paintings by Bellini, one with Rembrandt's, and one with Frans Hals's work sat opened at different pages on the dresser, in front of the wall-sized mirror, so sometimes it was *Doge Loredan*, or *The Anatomy Lesson*, and sometimes *The Laughing Cavalier* looking at me while I was brushing my hair. The chiffonier was packed with my dowry, which my parents had accumulated each year of my life until I was twelve and Dad went to prison. There were embroidered sheets, table covers, Persian rugs, blankets and soft throws for armchairs, crocheted things. With each bolt that loosened the bed frame from the headboard, one shelf from another, one part of the dresser from another, I felt emptier. It felt as if God was undoing my memories, taking my right to rest in my house. Like birds who had spent half of a spring building their nest of still frozen twigs and leaves, only to abandon it before the fledglings had learned how to fly, so were we on that night. Do birds ever return to abandoned nests?

The last night in our house we slept on the floor on mattresses like refugees, for despite the warning to leave our remaining possessions behind, we each gave away or sold what we could to anyone we could. We polished the floor one last time, and the floorboards, painted brown-red, smelled fresh and welcoming in a way, in a humbling, penitent way, as if to beg us to look closely at the foundation before looking up into the air of nowhere where we will go. I left some journals and most of my books, along with some clothes that I loved, to Aurora, and gave away the rest of my books to other friends. For the long journey ahead I kept a volume of poetry by Eminescu, my dictionary, and my poetry manuscript. That last night I was so deep into my own world, I didn't notice anyone. It was a sort of death, an unmerciful death, for I had to be awake through it and I had to see its aftermath. Late into the night we all sat on the porch and hid our tears from each other in the darkness, I think from exhaustion and not from reticence. My sister wanted a last trip to the attic so she went with a lit candle by herself, in her own world. Who knows the childhood games or the memories of fresh apples she remembered?

Now we stand here awaiting the accountant. A few crows shriek in the apple tree, the one that Tanti Jana said was cursed because the priest's daughter buried her newborn child beside its roots. The crows seem to claw at the tree, or am I imagining things? I wonder how people will refer to our house from now on: "Bugan's house"? In our villages people have been living and dying on the same plots of land for so many generations, no one I met could really count back. We are known to each other by the village, by the part of the village we are from: "Ion by the river," "Ioana by the forest." When people marry farther than one hundred kilometers away, the entire village assesses the "foreign" wedding rituals and traditions. Even if the land has belonged to the government since the 1960s, people haven't forgotten their own plots, and everyone has managed to keep a few hectares so that vineyards have been part of families since time immemorial. Bunicu Neculai's wine with its thick tannin taste is known as Butnaru wine, by his last name, to everyone around here.

The accountant shuffles through the green gates slowly. As he approaches the five of us, he takes off his cap. This morning Mom filled the bathtub with water and kissed the walls in insane, nonsensical gestures. Dad paced in the garage alone. I went to have one more look at the rockets and the stars Mom painted in the winter kitchen where my sister and I dreamed of being astronauts and navigated ourselves in loud daydreams along the gold contours of spaceships. Loredana went to her bedroom and sat there in a corner, on the floor, crying. In the hall, I notice how the spaces under our family portraits, which have now come off the walls for good, have retained the original shade of blue limewash. When the man extends his hand for the keys, I only notice his white cuff and the silver cuff link. As my skin touches his I look into his eyes; he looks down.

Now we leave the yard, our house locked to us. He goes on his way and we trudge with our suitcases to Bunicu Neculai's house, where we will spend the last of the summer while we wait for our passports to arrive and for our departure date from the American Embassy. Cătălin walks with us not quite understanding what is happening. His is a child's deep sadness. We find ourselves unable to acknowledge it, not because we don't think he is big enough to experience what we see in his expression, but perhaps because it is too painful for us. He is leaving the only house he knows, and who can guess the magical corners that will stay in his memory?

*

Bunicu Neculai doesn't understand why we have all moved in with him, but he enjoys the fresh food and having us around. He takes my brother's toy gun and shoots around the house, probably wrapped in his war memories. Cătălin's gun shoots little white balls that stray all over the kitchen. Often Bunicu asks me to turn off the pig, which is the light. Sad as his state of mind is, there is a merciful quality to his faulty memory; I have a feeling he will always remember our being young but will not remember our leaving.

We place a wall-sized map in the kitchen next to the red-brownish cupboard that I have known since I was born. There we mark România and then America in vibrant red, and Dad draws an arrow from home to the Great Lakes. Bunicu sometimes sits and looks at the map lost in thought, but we haven't a clue what goes on in his mind. Or so we think until one day when he takes my hand in his and leads me to the map, where he draws an imaginary line along the red one, from here to there, and says, "Before you go there, make me an altar on the cupboard, where I will pray for you."

There are moments in one's life that will never be touched by forgetting or newness or excitement. This is one of them. Bunicu takes the icon of Saint Nikolas, his namesake, the patron saint of sea travelers, places it on the table next to a bunch of grapes made by Bunica, in crochet, takes the oil candle off its place on the wall, and sends me outside for flowers. He sits at the table with his moist blue eyes watching carefully as I dust the cupboard and the altar objects. I arrange everything, including a handful of incense he has from church, in a display, then the gladioli from Titi's garden in a vase next to the altar. We both make the sign of the cross. He is aware that we are leaving, I understand this, so he returns to the life he had known: prayer, flowers, and the memory of his wife. Bunicu will die a happy man, for he knows the order and importance of things. He and this land belong together with their mutual memories and with God. He built his house of straw long before he began forgetting the present.

*

Summer blesses us with hot days and cool evenings. We set up mattresses on Bunicu's porch, where we sleep listening to the crickets sing in the grass. At night the sky is far above us, filled with millions of stars, which I try to count to help myself sleep.

"See those over there clouding into the Milky Way," Loredana says. "You try counting them or, better yet, imagine falling into the stars. What would it be like if we suddenly lost gravity and fell through all those stars? Do you think it's cold up there?"

"Bunica Anghelina used to say that the stars are the souls of people and the sky is the heaven where we go after we die. It doesn't seem so far from here, does it? Do you remember all those times she talked to us like that?"

Meanwhile, the fireflies strike their own sparks closer to us, under the grapevines, under the quince tree, into the pear tree. Cătălin pets Bunicu's dog. Mom and Dad talk themselves to sleep on the other side of the porch. We are ensconced again in the vault of roses that have grown all over the house ever since I can remember. This is again a magical time, perhaps made more so by the fact that we know for certain we will never sleep in this house, on this porch, again. Maybe this is why we are up at first light when the rooster announces the passing of time. "*Mînă caii*, Neculai," I tell myself again, but this time I want to go up dusty roads into memory.

*

Dad makes us practice English from our school notebooks during the day, but all I can say is, "Hello. My name is Carmen. I am sorry, I do not speak English. How do you do?"

Dad never bothers to study with us. I have a feeling he imagines that dogs really do run around with bagels on their tails in America and, moreover, they speak Romanian. He keeps telling us that the Americans found a sponsor for us so quickly, surely they will wait for him with honors and a big house to celebrate his fighting for human rights.

"Americans, Carmenuțo, will give us a big villa and a nice Chrysler and they will treat me with respect, like a hero. You might be sorry to leave but you will go to Harvard to study and we will forget this misery. Look how they treat us here, sending us out of our own house. There is nothing here for you. You should forget this place once we are out."

This is such strange territory to me, this imagining of trumpets and welcomes in America, that I have a difficult time visualizing it. I can only go as far as being in an airplane for the first time, so my fantasies are limited to being weightless, up in the sky, from where I will see the Atlantic. This gives me butterflies in my stomach. The rest is so vague, I prefer to go back to the stork nest in the garden and see her prepare for migration. Bunica once explained migration and homesickness to me, and it's easier to imagine homesickness than to visualize an American welcome. The quiet thrill, however, as I practice my English, is that one day I will be able to read Shakespeare in the original and again hear *Measure for Measure*, this time in its own tongue. Would it mean the same as it meant on the Iași Radio Drama? Would it be as intense as when I first heard it in Romanian? How long will it take until I will be able to read novels and poems in English? Will I ever be able to do that? But this is also a truly faraway thought.

Goodbye, My Village, October 1989

Throwing us out of our house has had an undesired effect on the Securitate: now they must travel to Bunicu Neculai's in order to keep an eye on us, so they look a lot more ridiculous than before. Bunicu's house can be approached only from the main road; there is no access to it from the backyard. This means that the Chinese-looking informer and the village policeman have to parade themselves the length of the village in front of gossiping old ladies who love to sit on their benches outside the gates spinning wool and feeling quite vociferously sorry for our family. There is certainly no shortage of condemning looks coming from them or from the old men. Each day the village policeman must pass in front of the house that belongs to my first-grade teacher and her husband, my geography teacher. They are both close to our family. I am not entirely certain that these people give the Securitate the customary "good day to you," for they also have strong alliances with my grandparents, both of whom had been playing big roles in the running of the village before the recent repression arrived in our backyards.

We will not be here long enough for the guards to take over other households in order to make observation posts for themselves, and people have got so used to them after all these years that they are no longer intimidated by their brown leather coats or their official-looking briefcases, despite seeing what happened to us. That's how things work in a small village. So now, when someone from the Securitate comes around, usually there is news to bring to us. This morning we are told to travel to Galați again in order to collect our passports.

*

I have never seen a passport before. Certainly I never have imagined owning one. When we had the pictures taken we felt a little like stars straight from the black-and-white movies of the 1940s. Our expressions came out anticipatory but not disastrously worried or too excited; in these photos we all look rather curiously calm and grounded. I know we all feel equally scared and starry-eyed about the Big Unknown Voyage.

The man at the passport office calls each of us to the window, where he looks at our faces, asks for our identity cards, which he takes away, and hands us the passports with looks of practiced disgust. At the end of the ritual he calls the entire family to the window and says solemnly, "You must know that if you say negative things about our great Communist Party or about anyone in the government, or if you dare tell anyone of anything that happened to you here because you committed propaganda against our regime, we will find you and kill you. The ditch will be your grave, wherever you are. We know where to find you. Our hand reaches far, Bugan. Do you understand, you criminal?"

Each of us replies, "Yes, I understand," knowing from the stories on Radio Free Europe and the Voice of America that what this man says is not metaphorical.

*

"Anyone want a last walk by the Danube?"

"Dad, this is a risky question after what we just heard. Nope, let's go straight home, forget the Danube."

"Carmen, you used to be a bit more romantic," chimes in Mom, clearly trying to cut through the tension of this one last death threat.

Loredana rolls her eyes at me. Well, okay, it's not so easy to explain our sense of humor these days. Dad, though he had some of his earliest youthful adventures in Galați, is not really in the mood for reminiscing. What I think he means by this invitation is, "Do any of you still want to stay here?"

*

What to put in one suitcase to take you to a whole new world? The *one* suitcase each of us is allowed is becoming a kind of house of straw. We pack and unpack frantically: this hand-knitted woolen sweater; this very old dress that is so full of memories it can be used as a housedress in exile; the red-cover selected poems by Eminescu that made me first think I can levitate and turn into a star among the millions spinning in the darkness; the overused, damaged dictionary; one embroidered tablecloth; the family portraits. Mom wants to get family and friends involved in our leaving, and over the weeks it dawns on me: this is her preparation for something akin to the afterlife. To her everything is a funeral, the details of which must be settled on her own terms. She already sees her absence, senses it in the village. It's all feverish and surreal.

October finds us packing our suitcases, visiting family to rehearse farewells, unpacking our suitcases. Mom and Dad bought me a very light, milky summer suit embroidered with the tiniest, barely noticeable silvery flowers around the neckline and at the hem. And they also bought me a shimmering dusty rose-pink suit that buttons all the way up to the chin; the skirt flows down way below my knees. We found the suits in a fashion shop, one we never used to visit since we never could afford or needed clothes so impressive. Little do I know that I will wear my milky-white suit at a Shakespeare festival in Stratford, Ontario, on a college trip to Canada, and I will feel out of place, out of time, in a good way. As I pack and unpack my clothes, I wonder if the Americans will think that we look ridiculous, like poor relatives from a forgotten corner of Europe. Tanti Săftica buys me a pair of red shoes, which she gives to me emotionally, saying, "I hope you will be like the girl from the story who danced her way in magic shoes, forgetting all of her sorrows."

Each of us is now also fitted with a blue lambskin winter coat for the cold season in America.

*

One thing I want to do alone is visit Bunica Anghelina's grave one more time. This is our final week. I avoid going near our house because I don't want to see the garden that had already been vandalized by the village thugs. We heard they tore through flowers and fruit trees, leaving branches fallen all over the place and dahlias smashed under the bolt of the grapevines. I take the long way around, up the streets nearest to the woods, behind the main roads. I walk up the hill to the cantor's house, turn onto the street behind, where Bunica's friend Maria lives next to the other women who make up the church choir, and I descend on the side of the woods, by the railroad tracks. Whenever we clean the graves, after Easter, Bunicu tells me he'd like to be buried next to Bunica, because on her side of the cemetery he will be able to hear trains as they pass by. "I love the trains when they whistle," he always says.

This time I take a candle and some incense, and I settle next to the blue wooden cross. I promise to return and tend the grave, and I cry so much, but even I don't believe half of what I am saying. Wherever we are going, I don't expect it will be a place from which return will be possible, so I act like a desperate relative at the bedside of someone who is about to die anyway. I lie cursing my own fate for having to lie, for I also feel sorry for myself, knowing I will never grow old here. After we buried Bunica Anghelina I turned around to look at the grave. The earth smelled fresh from being torn and turned and thrown over her, and I swore I saw her soul rising peacefully, like a white vapor or like fog, hovering gently above the hundreds of flowers we left with her. She always told me that souls breathe themselves out of their graves and join God in heaven, so I must have thought this is what happened.

"Goodbye, *bunicuța mea*. I am sure there will be sky over America, too, and I will look for you there."

*

The last walk with Aurora is more tense and artificial than I expected.

"I am not coming to the railway station to say goodbye to you tomorrow," she says, "because I want to remember you here. I have been more silent since you told me you were leaving because I need to survive this, I need new friends. Sorry, Carmen, I don't know how to say goodbye to you. I never thought this would happen. I thought we'd live near each other all of our lives and our children would play together."

Now I hate her but I cannot say that it's not my fault for leaving her or explain that it is easier for her to remain in a familiar place with everyone still around. I say, "Let's have one more walk around the park and one more cake, then I will leave you at home and walk back to Bunicu's alone. Remember, we are leaving in the morning from the north train station in Tecuci but we will spend a whole day in București before boarding the night train to Rome, so I will still be here for a while."

Why do people say such ridiculous things? Does it matter that I will be in the country for one more day? Maybe not to her, but I asked Sorin in a letter to meet me at the railway station in București on October 31 sometime in the early afternoon, and I hope he will be there.

*

Paler but beautiful, this morning's sun shines with a kind of nostalgia. Bunicu sits in the garden holding on to Cătălin's toy gun looking dreamy or sleepy, I am not sure which. He wears his black suit, his white shirt, and his hat. There is a pool of light around him. The five of us are buzzing with the last preparations, the closing of our suitcases, sounds of zippers and small keys turning in small locks, belts being tightened around the luggage. I bring a small bouquet of flowers to his altar and place it in the water, believing that he will pray for us. Tanti Săftica is here with fresh bread, fried chicken legs, and boiled eggs for the road. Yesterday, Bunicu, in and out of his forgetting, gave Dad a flask of his plum brandy, which we will keep for our first celebration. Titi arrives to collect us by car, to take us to the railway station in Tecuci, where Mom's sister and her husband, and other relatives and friends, will come to say goodbye.

After the suitcases are ready, we return to the yard to say goodbye to Bunicu and everyone else gathered there. Neighbors from all sides of the house are crowded in a circle in the yard, all of Tanti Săftica's family, Mom's school friends, our teachers, people from around the village. Everyone is crying so loudly that the collective sound is that of keening.

Mom cannot control herself and says, "This is our funeral, Nelu. Why do you take me away from my home? Why do you take me away from my father? You destroyed my life with your politics. I hate you!"

She pounds on Dad's chest with both of her fists while everyone wails. My mother is the labor and the fruit of this village. People love her and respect her. She is one of a few girls to graduate from high school and become a good teacher, then to follow it up with running the village café and the large grocery store in Iveşti. In our terms she is a career woman who has a rooted life in her family and her community. Truth be told, her ambitions have never leapt higher than to walk the length of our village and be greeted warmly by everyone. Awkward as her scene-making is, she is to be forgiven, allowed to make her grief manifest, for only God knows where we are headed.

What none of us knows today is that a few years from now, in Michigan, she will earn a nursing degree with nearly perfect grades and she will specialize in working with patients with Alzheimer's disease, probably from a subconscious desire to feel closer to Bunicu Neculai in his forgetfulness.

Bunicu stands up and speaks through the haze of Alzheimer's. "You must go with your husband. It is your duty to follow your family. I will pray for you all. You go now." He kisses her and he kisses us, making me proud to know that my *bunicu* can set us free from this grief.

In Tecuci the railway station is crowded with our friends and family. There are plenty of tears and goodbyes, and many promises to write. I search the crowd for Aurora in vain. As the train pulls away, we follow the trail of hands and handkerchiefs, not believing that this is the long goodbye. Well, goodbye, my village. "*Mînă caii,* Neculai," I say to myself again, pretty certain that none of the roads will be dusty or small or recognizable from here on.

*

The leave-taking in Bucureşti is mine alone, I think, despite the fact that there are family friends waiting for us here as well. Mine is Sorin. We have a few hours before the night train to the border. As the train approaches the station, I search for Sorin and do not see him. Dad's friends arrive slowly, we store the luggage, we talk with them, I search for Sorin. Did he get my letter? Is this it, an unopened letter? Or did the Securitate censor it? I am walking up and down the platform alone, restless, when a hand touches my shoulder and a bouquet of pale chrysanthemums brushes my cheeks.

"Do you think we can go to the museum?"

"Let's ask Dad. We have a few hours and everyone was talking about going into town for a bit. Dad wants to take us along the trail of his demonstration to show us what happened in 1983."

Maybe the leave-taking in Bucureşti also belongs to Dad.

"Here's the morgue parking lot where I slept before dawn. I told the night guard I came to collect a member of the family who died here, and he left me alone after he offered his condolences. In the morning, when the traffic was heavy, I went to find the quickest exit onto Piaţa Romană. Let's walk there now and I will tell you what happened."

My father is now animated. His cheeks are turning pink and he demands our undivided attention as he relives his experience.

"I never, ever, felt happier in my entire life," he says, without realizing the pain he is creating in our hearts as he speaks.

"Not even when I was born?" I ask him.

"Carmen, there are things that bear no comparison. This was the happiest moment in my life, you must know this. I was driving in the main square, all the traffic stopped, people burst out of all the buses and trams, I was throwing manifestos at them out the window with one hand, driving with the other, my soldering gun on the dashboard to create the impression that I was armed. I made it pretty close to the American Embassy, hoping their cameras would catch a view of me and spread the news that we were protesting in this country. You should have seen the excited and horrified looks of hundreds of people. There is nothing like it! I gave these people a jolt into courage, you understand this? For your country!"

But the day we are leaving this country, the impressive piazza is quiet, as people continue to starve peacefully and go to sleep in darkness. The Securitate has frightened everyone into silence, and those like my father are being pushed out like garbage into trains that take them and their families into the murky territories of nowhere. Why? It is because the people who gawked at the impressive placards mounted on my father's car, those who took and read his manifestos, were too scared to join him in full-fledged protest. I feel both sorry for him and angry with this country in which the most common sentiment is fear.

*

"Dad, can we wander through the art museum one last time?"

"Okay."

Sorin and I do our best to stray away from my family so we can be alone briefly. These are our final stolen moments. If our fate was any different I would allow myself to think more about what might happen between the two of us. I drift through rooms, in front of paintings, more quiet than I had imagined. I think I imagined lots of kissing and crying. There is nothing I can say to impress on him, so I think to myself that permanent leave-taking is a bit tiring and artificial: it's mostly like waiting for. a late train. Then Sorin grabs my hand in front of a Renaissance painting of Saint Mary that is on loan from Italy and says, "Swear to me here, in front of this painting, that you will wait for me and be mine forever. I'll come to find you wherever you are, someday I will. Please tell me you will wait. I love you!"

I cannot believe this, I am dizzy. "Yes, I will wait, all my life if I have to, I promise."

I make this promise easily, almost mechanically, for I imagine it would have been a natural thing to happen to us if I had stayed. The bouquet of chrysanthemums in my hands suddenly feels heavy and I want to throw it up in the air. Now I really don't want to go anywhere.

*

More exhausted than emotional, we crowd into the train covered by welcome darkness, Cătălin in my arms, and we sleep through the morning with the hands of our friends in our minds' eyes, me with Sorin's black eyes fixed in a hopeful goodbye. At the border, at Stamora Moravița, the train comes to a sudden halt. We are searched and taken onto the platform, from where we watch the train cross the border. We spend the day and the following night on stone benches guarded by soldiers and dogs. My father is searched in a small office all alone, and when he emerges putting his clothes on, his face is red, his eyes are red. I will never know what happened to him in there. The Securitate confiscates my poetry manuscript in a last act of pillaging stupidity. What hurts the most is the way the guards feel through the lining of our coats, sink their hands into each piece of clothing. No one tells us why we are being held at the border.

When we are finally on the next train, when we finally cross the border, I feel only hatred for my country: this was the final goodbye. Now I know I will never want to return. I have nothing left untouched other than Sorin's bouquet and my secret, both of which I carry all the way to Florence, where I throw away the flowers and tell my family that Sorin asked me to wait for him and I said I would. Gently, very gently, my family tells me that sometimes the most beautiful, true, and innocent promises cannot be kept, but that they will allow me to write to him and make a try. I will not see Sorin again. Our family's

Big Unknown Voyage begins with Bunicu's plum brandy biting our tired, dry mouths as we cross the border. Then the first sips of Coca-Cola from a bottle that a Romanian expatriate shares with us on a train between Belgrade and Trieste. When he offers it to us, Dad asks him to drink first, convinced he is a Securitate man attempting to poison us. It turns out that he is just an emigrant visiting his mother in România; he is settled in Australia, where there are all sorts of crazy things walking upon the earth.

Returning to Rome, 2006

I find my way as one does in a dream, intuitively, to Pensione Dina. This time I am with my own Italian family, Alessandro's parents. We turn left on a side exit from Roma Termini, walk right along the street with small, cheap, dirty shops, go left at the first corner, and head two streets down before turning left again. There is a slight hesitation: the street is three blocks from the first left turn, not two. Alessandro's father offers to ask one of the hotel porters for directions and we are disappointed, for the man knows a Hotel Diana, sending us on a street I do not remember. Both in-laws venture that maybe in my memory Diana could be Dina, and I think that by some trick the place no longer exists, as many places I have been to no longer exist. I have no recollection of street names, only a feel for the streets, and I begin reaching for the feelings, walking almost blindly. I jump when I see the sign. We step into the large hall to find the same dirty white curtain half-fallen from its high rod—did it really fall like this and stay frozen, as in my mind, for seventeen years? The gray marble and cement walls, the wood-and-glass elevator, the same neon sign. And, just as it was seventeen years ago, the same stack of maps on the counter that my brother, six years old at the time, could not reach.

Some memories are as strong as flesh and blood, and you don't notice until you hurt yourself, until something stings you. I try to explain this in English to my parents-in-law and then I reach further, into Italian, while they reach further into English, and then I understand that there is no need for many words.

I say to both, "Many years ago, we were blind with wonder here," and Alessandro's father translates for my mother-in-law, "*acciecati dalla meraviglia.*" I tell them about the view from our room at Pensione Dina, especially in the mornings, when the bells called from the hills and everyone opened their windows, speaking with their neighbors from the windowsills. We were on one of the top floors, knowing the morning by the noise of the trams and church bells. We awoke to women and men rattling their consonants in a tongue in which we knew only "*buongiorno.*" I remember opened windows all along the street, colored shutters, all opened, people in window frames.

We arrived at Pensione Dina in the night. After two days' traveling by train from București to Moravița to Belgrade, Trieste, Venice, and Florence, filled with curiosity and exhaustion, we found ourselves at the end of the track, where all rail tracks end. Before traveling to Michigan, we were to spend two weeks in Rome undergoing medical and immigration checks, and taking an introductory course on American culture, in which we learned that each American has a checkbook, and it doesn't matter how sad you feel, when someone asks you, "How are you today?" you must always answer, "Fine, thanks!" At București we had said our farewells to family and friends, leaving them in the hands of the Securitate interrogators. As we crossed the border we looked at the fresh footsteps on the earth outside the window: those were fresh tracks made by fugitives, probably while the border guards were busy minding us. When we crossed into Italy, the train company switched to Trenitalia and the language changed to bright-sounding words in which stations were announced slowly all the way to Roma Termini.

It was a long walk from the platform to the station entrance, and I remember all of us dizzied by colored shop displays, the noise of the world, rumbling in various languages. My father and I left my mother, sister, and brother in the station and set about finding Pensione Dina with the directions we had from the American Embassy. The foray was easy—almost a good omen—and Dad and I brought everyone to the gray building, climbed the stairs, turned in our documents, and found ourselves with a set of keys and a map of Rome, sometime past midnight.

Now, in the welcoming heat of May 2006, I pay my respects to that first night in Rome by taking a photo of a bewildered man behind the reception desk. I am dying to call my parents in Grand Rapids to tell them about this trip, though I must wait until my sister finishes her night shift in the hospital and Mom finishes her sixteen-hour shift, to make sure I do not get the answering machine. I don't speak enough Italian to explain to my in-laws that I am retracing my life, or that this will be the starting point of a book I will write about my family's exile to Michigan. I smile, Alessandro's mother smiles, the man at the reception desk smiles.

We head over to Santa Maria Maggiore, where, stunned by ancient history, whirled into a new civilization, seventeen years ago we stumbled into Mass. Alessandro's father haggles over the price of a rosary, which I buy for my mother. (We are Orthodox, but approximation will do.) A Calabrian man, he loves the relaxed lifestyle of the south and the long conversations in shops and at bazaars. Below the steps of Santa Maria Maggiore, a young man selling trinkets speaks to me in perfect English until my father-in-law intervenes, questioning him about his place of birth and the price of rosaries.

"For my daughter, you give discount, no?" he says, waving his hands happily.

The twenty-four-euro rosary soon becomes ten, when the haggling grows in a beautiful fast language until the price is set at nine euros for a set of Venetian rose glass beads with a small iron cross at the end. This time I don't feel like an immigrant or like a tourist—in a strange way, I belong here, having another memory to add to the ones from many years ago. We go into the church, where my father-in-law sits while Alessandro's mom and I look at the paintings, at the marble statue of a pope. I retrace my path from the other side of my Romanian border. When I learn Italian, I will tell my in-laws how I discovered piazzas and fountains for the first time, how I tasted pistachio ice cream, and how I made a set of footprints in their country on the way to America.

Afterword:
The Files, 2010–2011

It is almost twenty-one years since our exile to America. About a year ago I applied for permission to study the files created on me by the Securitate, from the archive of dossiers kept on my family. I was told that I have one passport dossier, but under the name Ion Bugan they have four dossiers, three about the times he spent in prison and one about his being under surveillance. This last "informative" dossier includes reports from various Securitate collaborators drawn from family, friends, and coworkers. The nature of the surveillance was "permanent."

I asked myself a lot of questions before deciding to take this trip to România. Will I find audiotapes of conversations we tried to drown in the noise of the kitchen? Will there be pictures of me kissing a certain boy in the park? Will I hear our voices from a quarter of a century ago? Should I take my husband and my son along? Is my grandparents' house still there, and does the stork still return to the tree stump? What about our house—will my peach tree still wait for me there? Will the Black Sea still talk to me as it did when I was a child? Will they say in the dossiers how they stretched my father on the wall on the *macavelă*, like the Vitruvian Man?

The day we boarded the plane for București, on July 18, 2010, I wasn't certain I had made the right decisions, to go and to take my little family with me. But my mom was waiting there already, having made the journey from the United States. My father is not interested in such files. I understand him. My sister does not want to see them, either, and I can see her point too. But I want to peer into our "second inheritance" because this is who we are, the "we who *we* say we are" and the "we who *they* say we are."

*

Mom on my arm, I am standing in the hallway of the CNSAS, an organization that collects documents created by the Securitate and makes them available to the public. There are displays of surveillance instruments in the hallways (old-style cameras, video cameras, and microphones), but I am not allowed to photograph them. Someone comes to take us into the reading room. Our desk fills with stacks of documents. I feel oddly as if I am sitting in a library, studying for an exam. I need a drink of water; my mouth is dry. I ask for water and think that maybe I should not have, maybe they will put something in it. I remember the room without windows at the Internal Ministry where they asked me to wait for my interview about seeing my father; I had a feeling something happened there. My mother tells me that I exaggerate. We find a picture of my twenty-six-year-old father. It's just head and shoulders, but you can see he is wearing a black suit. His hair is thick and dark, brushed back, with curls falling on his forehead; his eyes are big and expressive. He has well-shaped lips, his cheeks are soft, he has a look that isn't quite a smile but isn't severe or scared either. Does he look relaxed? It's not possible. The picture is stapled to the inside cover of his 1961 prison dossier from Aiud.

Then there is the dossier of the 1983 demonstration. I find the pictures of the typewriter, the laboratory examinations of the keyboard, my parents' fingerprints. There is a map of România on which the places where my parents spread their manifestos are marked. There are hundreds of handwritten reports by people who were surprised to find anti-Communist propaganda in their mailboxes and who cowered and ran straight to the Securitate with them. On one page something makes me jump: a picture of my grandmother's feet, with her crinkly socks and plastic slippers, standing on the edge of the hole where, in a white plastic barrel, sits the typewriter wrapped in a towel. I bend over and look.

"Carmen, your father said he buried the typewriter at the back of the house. Where is it?" The voice of the interrogator comes back to me across the years.

And then I look in the picture harder and harder, for my feet, because I was there and I answered the question, protecting my parents. But my feet aren't there, just as I don't have a dossier at CNSAS but rather one at the National Passports Archive, where two ladies laugh and say, "You think you're going to find more than the paperwork for the passports? Why do you want to waste your time?"

My mother looks around the reading room, which is filled with people. I follow her eyes. There is a sense of quiet resignation over lost lives mixed with a sense of pride: all of us there fought back or were part of the lives of those who fought back.

After two days of quick reading and writing requests for photocopies, my mother and I are back in the heat wave of a dirty and desolate Bucureşti. Many years are missing from the archives, and much information about how my father was followed from the late 1970s until 1983. There is nothing about our family in 1988 in our last year in România, when we lived under house arrest. How is this possible? I am told that these records are still classified or lost and damaged, and if they ever become available I will be called to return to Bucureşti to read them. But I still have volumes to deal with—and it's knowledge that comes as a sort of exile from Eden. Am I worthy of gaining this knowledge? Am I entitled to have this knowledge because I am a part of it? Will my life make sense without this knowledge now that I know it exists?

We are going to Tecuci, Drăgăneşti, the mountains, and the Black Sea, all in two weeks. At Tecuci I find the courthouse where my parents were forced to divorce. In the central park, which is now rebuilt, I meet an old English-language teacher from when I was thirteen years old. He tells my uncle and my aunt that he has something on his conscience that he has carried for twenty years; he needs to see me about it. He talks about how he and all the other teachers watched from the schoolroom as the guards changed shifts in the church bell tower across the street at seven in the evening while my father was imprisoned. He saw that I was kept home from school by the interrogators. One day, he remembers, I was walking on the church side of the street looking at the school across the road. He didn't know where I was going but knew that I was not allowed to go to school. He says that he did not find in himself the courage to say hello to me and say a good word, say, for example, that my father was a good man and that I should be proud of him, or say that he felt sorry for me. His confession is about an act of kindness that did not take place, about a government that scared its own people so much they could no longer talk.

"I wrote a play," he says, "and would like you to read it. It has something of this in it. I carried that image of you in my head for twenty years. I am sorry I could do nothing for you."

I say it's okay; it was like that then with everyone.

Our house now belongs to another priest—it keeps returning to the ownership of priests. In 1997 we returned for a few days to say goodbye to Bunica Floarea as she was dying of cancer. It was winter, and we stayed with relatives who fought with each other to host us. We danced a *hora* in Titi's living room and drank wine that Tanti Săftica had saved year after year, for each year that we were gone, in the desperate hope that one day we would drink from each bottle together. This is how she survived our being away from her. Bunica talked to us and caressed our cheeks; she had become so tender and weak in her final days, it was hard to recognize her. We all sat at the edge of her bed, my mother curled next to her, as we did before in our own house. On that occasion my parents repossessed the house and donated it to the village church. It has been a parochial house ever since, though the priests with their families have come and gone. The current priest is on vacation and I do not have a chance to go inside, to walk about, to touch the walls. The door of this garden remains locked.

Sofica walks from across the street in the same way she did twenty-some years ago. We embrace, we sit on her porch, and we talk. She recalls that I used to climb up a ladder on the side wall to the attic where they kept hay and I played my guitar there. Her husband says that they saw on television the other night how my father was tortured. He is talking about a documentary on anti-Communist resistance for which my father gave an interview some years ago. They give me pink gladioli. I take off my necklace and place it around Sofica's neck.

A layer of cement has been placed over the old green paint of the outside walls of my grandparents' house. Though there are lots of flowers everywhere and the vegetable garden glows with abundance, the rosebushes that once climbed the walls are gone, and so is the tree stump that was the stork's house. The house and garden seem to suffer from a kind of silence: the silence of our not being there. It is the silence of a childhood that now I fear is dying with every step that I take on the bald part of the yard. What am I looking for here but the breathing of everyone, the warm scent of bread baking, the grapes, the animals, us children learning the language of happiness, which we shall never forget? I have dreamed so many nights during the past twenty years about this house where everything magic happened. In many dreams the house was crumbling, but in others I was playing, searching through the doors of the rose-embossed cupboards of Bunica's *iatac*, finding old letters smelling of dust and time.

Among the very few younger people left in my village since the Revolution of 1989 I find Aurelia, one of my best friends from when I was about six years old. After trying a career in the city she returned to her parents' house, where she opened a small grocery store. It is our grade-school teacher who tells me to go next door and see Aurelia. I would love to spend a few days with her talking about our lives. She was always the best at everything in school and we had delightful times playing together on and around the kilometer marker, which happened to be posted just outside her house: Tecuci: 8 km. Hide-and-seek, jump the marker, sit on the marker, put things on top of the marker occupied most of our afternoons. Her parents come out of the house when they hear the commotion outside and they sob. They tell me how much Aurelia cried when I left. By now the entrance to the store is filled with people and we move with the crowd into the street. We take group pictures, we don't really know what to say, and I leave heavyhearted as if I have just started something I will not be able to finish.

Tanti Săftica sits up in bed and when I ask her she wobbles into the next room to find old photographs. We talk about them, she gives me as many as I want to take, and it seems to me as if I am going back in time much farther than my early childhood: here's a photo of my grandfather with his cart and horse, and here's one of my grandmother when she was young. And here's one of Tanti Săftica when she was young. What a thief time is, how it steals the freshness of our skin, the color from our hair, how it steals our sight.

*

One evening when we sit down for dinner with our hosts in the mountains, the television suddenly quiets our conversation with the news that the graves of the Ceaușescus have just been exhumed at the request of their family. I am in România digging through the archives of my family the same week as the tyrant is being exhumed in order to be put to rest properly. In a flashback I see my family at Christmas 1989 watching on TV how Ceaușescu and his wife were shot. It was our first month in America. Peace to peace.

At the Black Sea, which I have not seen in over twenty years, thousands of dead fish of all sizes lie on the beach and in the water. There is a heat wave but everyone stands at the edge of the sea looking at the water in disbelief. The few who venture in step on or are bitten by a poisonous fish and are taken to the hospital by ambulance. I have a fight with my husband, who wants to go in the water with our young son. My son sits on the sand just where the waves come to touch his skin, and I feel that I cannot breathe.

What is it that makes people want to go back to their homeland after so many years? Curiosity? Maybe a hope that they can make sense of their lives with the help of some government files? Maybe it is nostalgia? I step into my old high school with my husband and my son.

At first the secretary laughs at me, saying, "What, you are nostalgic for your school years?" But then she understands what I mean when I tell her how long I have been gone.

I sit in my chair at my desk and look for a sign, which I do not find. Instead I stumble on memories of the bouquets of snowdrops Sorin used to hide inside, behind my pencils and books. Before I emigrated, and despite the Securitate following us everywhere, there was at least a promise of love. How much we tried to be together, and yet how much history has pushed our story to the side. How unimportant this seems now. How different my life had been. I asked around about Aurora but no one knows where she had gone.

*

At the international airport in București I say goodbye to my country with a sense of relief. A visit such as this tangles one up in knots. The last night that we spent on the Black Sea, a cousin took us for a late drive to a monastery so close to the beach you could hear the waves. My mother, my husband, and I protested, thinking it was rude to wake the monks and the nuns at eleven o'clock only so that we could go in and pray. But they opened the gates, turned on the lights, lit the candles in the chapel, and waited for us while we took turns kissing the icons. At the end of the visit, my mother went into the shop and bought a year's worth of prayer for the whole family: she paid the monks and the nuns to mention our name to God at their morning and evening prayers.

That night the sky was filled with shooting stars. My son squealed with happiness every time he saw one. I am pretty sure everyone made a wish. My mother says that the monastery visit gave her a sense of closure. Me, I kiss her goodbye and promise to see her and Dad in the States. I don't have a sense of closure; my feelings skid across the night sky—stars and sorrow.

*

It is May 2011. I am in a library in Geneva, Switzerland, at a small desk looking over a sunny courtyard filled with trees in flower. On my desk are two white envelopes containing a few pages each, minuscule fragments of the files I recently received from the National Council for the Study of the Archives of the Securitate. It took almost a year for the photocopies to arrive. Somewhere close by a photocopier squeaks, someone is tapping the floor with one foot, someone shuffles and taps his keyboard. In the envelopes I find the sound of courtrooms, prison chains, betrayals, and the ever-present smell of lindens under which my parents undoubtedly talked most of their first years of marriage and under which we all huddled to talk about fears and hopes in the last eleven months we spent in România.

In these two white envelopes, the few pages from the secret files kept on my father from 1960 until 1989 groan under the pressure of compressed time. I chose them quickly, impulsively, intuitively, my heart beating so hard and fast I could feel its thumping in my ears. My father spent a total of twelve years in the worst Romanian prisons and forced labor camps because he praised the democratic values of the West while openly criticizing the structure and philosophy of communism. I ask myself: was he really that dangerous? In one file they say he represented a threat to communism because he talked with admiration of how Americans went to the moon.

In one of the anti-Ceaușescu pamphlets typed by my father sometime in February 1981, which I found collected by the Securitate and placed in his 1983 penal dossier, he called everyone to strike until demands were met: five-day working week; forming of a free syndicate; returning the land to the peasants; permission to start small private businesses; permission to travel abroad for pleasure, work, or for joining family who escaped or was exiled; freeing of all political dissidents; bettering the infrastructure and transportation of food to villages and towns, especially in the remote areas of the country; better pension schemes. In some letters he sent anonymously from various parts of the country he calls Ceaușescu a tyrant and urges people to take to the street to demand their rights. He points out the self-aggrandizing behavior of Ceaușescu, how he used the land of the country as private property where he went hunting. I remember how one school day everyone was crowded into buses and taken to the forests in our districts where Ceaușescu went hunting for boar. We were made to wear traditional peasant costumes, kept inside the buses starving and without water most of the day, and when the helicopter flew with Ceaușescu and his hunting crew over the meadow where we were parked, we were all taken out and made to dance a *hora*. Later on yet, when we heard the hunting dogs, we were made to sing at the top of our lungs so that Comrade Ceaușescu and his friends would hear the song of the happy peasants. My own memories fuse with my father's protest: it is now more than thirty years since he wrote out his demands. My father's typing runs over the margins, his language betrays anger and impatience, his demands are numbered and the prose is wordy, yet written in a hurry, the faded type spilling over the edges of the paper: he is a desperate man fighting for a desperate cause. I see that he refers to Lech Walesa as an example; he wants to show people that in România too, everyone must stand up and build a better life.

Someday soon, I would like to use these dossiers as a guide and retrace my father's second failed escape from România, through Bulgaria, all the way to the frontier with Turkey, where he learned that the Iron Curtain was made of a double, not a single, fence and he was sent back to the Romanian prisons after he was showered with bullets. They have kept the maps, the photos of his binoculars and compass. I have a hint from the files and from him of what it must have been like to walk into blinding February snows with lemons, chocolate, and cognac in his rucksack to the border between oppression and freedom, but I want to retrace his journey for my own education.

The Securitate, the Romanian secret police of the Cold War era, spied on people by all means possible. They used family members and friends who were either bribed or threatened to get them to report. The structure of the organization was intricate. With the help of a large hierarchy of militarily ranked staff who trained, informed, and spread untrue stories about protesters in order to discredit their character, the Securitate gained access to the most intimate details of personal lives. Photos were taken of suspect or threatening people like my father;

there was audio and video surveillance, censorship of correspondence. Files were kept on family life, work and travel habits, tastes. They employed all of these methods to spy on my father.

My brother, my sister, my mother, and I were objects of surveillance during the last five years we lived in România. And there was intimidation, threats from which it is difficult to recover. By the time we left the country I have no idea if we could have recognized within ourselves the difference between thoughts or feelings we had spontaneously and those we created to display for our protection. I remember now Mom's remark: "I have stopped having feelings. I am no longer able to *feel*." This is a bewildered look at oneself, a recognition that such isolation, pressure, not knowing which of our friends were friends and which were informers, the atmosphere in which we could not tell illusion from hope, made us all just stop feeling altogether.

*

I open the envelopes to translate the few pages from these files. To me, now, they also represent a magical way into the past. Here is a story I typed, when I was about eleven years old, about an old woman who had three tall but rather dumb sons; it was confiscated along with the buried typewriter. I sit with the photocopy of this story in my hands and remember how I first came to love words on paper—that first typewriter stirred the young writer in me. In one file, Lieutenant Ghețu, who was in charge of spying on my father at the beginning of my parents' marriage, notes on June 1, 1973, "The situation of the objective is as follows: he has two young children for whom he cares very much. He also loves his wife, who is very beautiful, as can attest those who know her." Where could I find a more perfect Mother's Day gift this year?

Zoom through a 1960 bar scene somewhere in the southwest of România where my father drinks beer with his friends and says he doesn't like communism, then zoom, a few flips of the files to a room in a prison where he is kept in solitary confinement because he tried to escape from prison. And then zoom to when he comes home with a little puppy in his arms for us children and has no idea someone is watching him. This is my lifeline into a different and yet familiar past. How could I not be glad?

*

It is fortuitous that I wrote *Burying the Typewriter* before the arrival of the files, for in them I also found the letter by which my natural grandfather Toader had renounced Dad as a son, refusing to receive his meager possessions (a blanket, some dishes, a green table, a bed painted green, a green metal washbasin, a desk, a chair, his wallet—the detailed list emerges from a handwritten file) when he was first taken to prison in 1961 for speaking against the government and for trying to run away from the country. Was the father's love weaker than the fear, possibly beatings, surely threats? Would I ever know the struggle in his heart? What gave some people the courage to resist, like my grandmothers did? What gave some people the certitude that if they bowed their heads, they would not be shamed anyway? And then I think of the solitude my father experienced when he saw his father's letter. Did he ask, "Oh, Father, why?"

I trace the contours of my grandfather's words with my fingers, trying to imagine. The records I have here have been numbered, renumbered, copied, recopied, erased. Much of the information has been destroyed, so I will never know the whole story. Had I had this knowledge before I wrote this book, perhaps the voice of the child would have been strangled.

So here, in this leap of time, the child speaking early in the book has no idea that there are secrets, sometimes evil secrets, and sometimes protective secrets whispering in the souls of family and friends, as sparrows nest and sing in the magical eaves of her grandparents' house. The child sings and leaps in the front room as she waits for her parents to assemble the first family tent in which they will all sleep on the shores of the Black Sea. As if the world was perfect. When I wrote the book I did not know what I know now, that the night my father came home drunk with the goose in his arms could have been the end of a day when he was called and harassed by the Securitate or a day when a good friend turned good informer asked him about his thoughts on the latest people's congress, a question that he answered pretty much, "Well, I don't care, only time will tell if we will live better lives or not," something later recorded neatly in a "Note of information," signed code-name "Savin."

What a blessing it is that I did not know these things! Without knowing what I know now from the files, I was able to remember the joy I truly experienced, a joy that has sustained me until now.

*

It is August 2011. I close the envelopes with their noises and sorrows. My husband, my son, and I are ensconced on the shores of Lake Annecy in France, stealing a final week of vacation before the birth of our second child. The child in my heart plays with Steluța, the mare, in a magical garden where a stork nests on a tree stump. Bunica tends her marigolds, Bunicu repairs the pigeons' nest, and Loredana taunts the turkey. Cătălin will be born a few years on. Time begins again.

Appendix: Archival Material

During the more than thirty years since the events described in this book took place, dates have moved in my memory across months and seasons. The files provide the actual dates for events that are important in the life of my family.

Out of about 1,500 pages that I was able to find at the archives of the CNSAS, I selected for the following appendix only a few. There are more dossiers missing, since the files contain references to material that was not given to me. Also, there are no records of many events I witnessed myself, either as an object of harassment or as an observer of my parents' ordeals with the Securitate. The excerpts included here from the 1971 informative dossier and the 1983 penal dossier illustrate the situation described in the memoir as follows:

1. The pages from the informative dossier for "Andronic" in 1971 show how my father, a political prisoner from 1961 until 1968, was also followed and harassed from the beginning of his marriage to my mother; my parents were married in 1969. The excerpt included here lists the various methods used to monitor my parents from the time I was one year old. It provides a context for the first half of the book, where I describe my childhood as full of innocence and happiness, clearly not knowing about my father's past or about my parents' troubles with the Securitate in their first years of marriage. This period begins with my parents living in Vrancea, where my sister and I were born, and continues through their move back to Drăgănești, where we lived with my grandparents and later built our new house.

2. The pictures of the mailboxes are just one example of the places where my parents spread anti-Communist propaganda and literature against Ceaușescu. The notes written on the pictures show the investigative work done by the Securitate in their effort to establish who typed the material found in the mailboxes. From this dossier it is

apparent that the Securitate was on the trail of my father from 1981 until his one-man protest against the government in the center of Bucureşti in 1983. I included the photos of the mailboxes to show just how closely the Securitate monitored any kind of unwelcome literature relating to the government.

3. The last section in the appendix is the transcript of the sentence given to my father for his protest against Ceauşescu. I included this to show that the trial was held in secret and that he did not have any chance to defend himself.

Additional information about the material that follows is to be found in the footnotes I have provided.

The Socialist Republic
of România

The Council for the
Security of State[1]

Access of Document:
Strictly Secret

Direction: Vrancea[2]

Service:

Section:

Office:[3]

Type of dossier:
Dossier of Informative
Surveillance

CODE NAME: Andronic

The surveillance/spying[4]
begins on 18 JAN 1971

The surveillance ends on........

Archival number....[5]

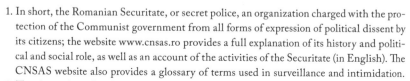

1. In short, the Romanian Securitate, or secret police, an organization charged with the protection of the Communist government from all forms of expression of political dissent by its citizens; the website www.cnsas.ro provides a full explanation of its history and political and social role, as well as an account of the activities of the Securitate (in English). The CNSAS website also provides a glossary of terms used in surveillance and intimidation.
2. The place where this dossier was initiated.
3. The various stamps indicate, with the appropriate signatures, the dates when the dossier or parts used to assemble this dossier were photocopied for the purpose of gathering information that justifies spying against my father. The dossier itself is structured in sections that include motives for opening a spying action against my father; an analysis of the threat he represents to the government; the various methods and people employed to spy on him; actual reports on him by various spies or people forced and trained to report on him; continual analysis of his personality, personal habits, travel habits, and psychological and emotional states; and continual assessment of the likelihood that he will express criticism of the government or attempt to run away from the country.
4. As included in this dossier; there are earlier ones.
5. There are various numbers written in pen or pencil on the cover page, probably indicating the number of the dossier itself as it was classified in various archives. They could also possibly indicate that there are other versions of this dossier: I noticed that parts to which the reader is referred for further information are not there, and there are many gaps in information.

214

The Surveillance
Dossier Comprises:[6]

—the materials that
show the reasons
for initiating the
surveillance and the
documents in which
the chief of the
investigation explains
his decision to continue
with surveillance
activities;

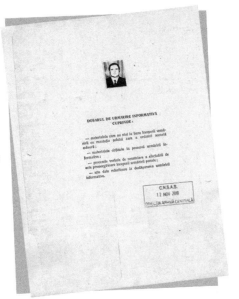

—the materials obtained
in the process of
surveillance;

—documents and
paperwork relating
to gathering of
evidence before a penal
surveillance;

—other data obtained in the course of surveillance.

CNSAS photocopy stamp

6. Photo of my father probably taken from the records office or his driver's license (circa 1970).

The Internal Ministry

The Vrancea
Securitate
Branch   Strictly secret

Unique copy

May 29, 1973   Approved

Signature and rank
of the officer who
approved this action

Handwritten note:
*at this date (Oct. 8,
1973) the mission was
reviewed by Mr....
who gave verbal
instructions.*

Signatures

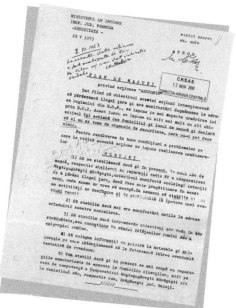

Plan of Measures Regarding
the Mission "Andronic"

Given the fact that the objective[7] of this action
has intentions to leave the country and manifests
unfriendly sentiments toward the regime of the
Socialist Republic of România, it is decided to
impose upon him a surveillance of the type D.U.I.[8]
This surveillance is necessary even more because
the objective changes his residence and place of
work often, and declares openly that he is not
afraid of the Securitate, which, he insists, cannot
harm him.

---

7. Ion Bugan.

8. D.U.I.: This is the most comprehensive type of secret police surveillance, reserved for the most dangerous political dissidents. It means that the person will have a surveillance dossier that could later serve in arrest and imprisonment. The "hostile" behavior mentioned here is simply my father expressing criticism of the regime, complaining to his family and friends about the general lack of freedom to speak and to travel, and saying things such as "this regime will collapse from within."

In order to carry this complicated mission to successful completion, it is hereby ordered:

Duties

1) To be established if now, at the new job, namely, the TV-radio repair shop in the Cooperative of Mărăşeşti, the objective manifests intentions of leaving the country illegally, if he is preparing for this, where it is that he would like to go. We should establish also what kind of activities he is likely to take up once abroad in case his escape is successful.

2) To be established if he still displays hostile behavior regarding our socialist system.

3) To be established if he indeed has any relatives or friends abroad.

4) Establish what kinds of methods he will be likely to use in case of planning an escape from the country.

5) Establish if he also now repairs TVs and radios privately, which is not authorized: this to be checked in the vicinity of the Cooperative and also around his residence in Drăgăneşti, the district of Galaţi.

6) Establish if he has any relations/friends likely to engage in similar behavior as the suspected objective.

In order to carry out these goals, the following duties will be imposed:

Measures/Duties

a) Since none of our informers from the Mărăşeşti network area know the objective, we will recruit and train an informer who will be directed around the objective.

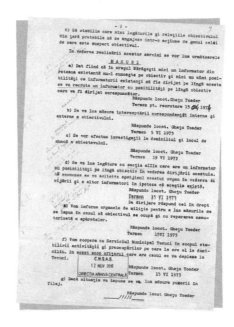

In charge, Lieutenant Gheţu Toader, term for recruiting, 15.04.1974

b) All correspondence of the objective will be intercepted.

In charge, Lieutenant Gheţu Toader, term 5.06.1973

c) There will be investigations at work and home of the objective.

In charge, Lieutenant Gheţu Toader, term 19.06.1973

d) There will be established a link with Section III, which has an informer with possibilities relating to the objective and the informer will be directed. The same section will be solicited for extra informers, assuming they have them.

In charge, Lieutenant Gheţu Toader, term 15.06.1973

Those who are in charge will be responsible for directing the informers.

e) The police will be alerted to monitor if the objective does private radio-TV work.

In charge, Lieutenant Gheţu Toader, term 15.06.1973

f) We will cooperate with the Tecuci Securitate branch to see what activities the objective carries out at home and what are his preoccupations. For this, the officer assigned to this case will travel to Tecuci.

In charge, Lieutenant Gheţu Toader, term 15.06.1973

g) If the situation makes it necessary we will put him in direct and complete surveillance of all of his travel.

In charge, Lieutenant Gheţu Toader

h) Because the objective does/did field work in his capacity of radio and TV repairman in the villages of and around Vultur and Măicăneşti we will continue to direct informers around the objective.

In charge, Lieutenant Gheţu Toader

Major Lupu Grigore[9]

Term of surveillance: Permanent[10]

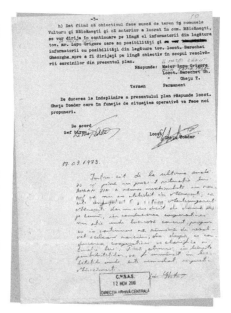

---

9. Other names written in pencil.

10. Below are more signatures, the CNSAS photocopy stamp, and a handwritten note dated September 17, 1973, advising following my father in Măicăneşti.

220

DOSSIER

Regarding BUGAN ION,

GUILTY OF:

Propaganda Against
the Socialist Regime,
article 166 paragraph 2
of the penal code[11]

11. Additional handwritten numbers and the CNSAS stamp. This dossier contains detailed
information regarding my parents' typing anti-Communist propaganda on the illegally
owned typewriter and distributing it all over România, as well as my father's anonymous
letters against Ceaușescu, which he posted from various towns and villages to all the
major publications, and finally his trial and sentence. The dossier of his incarceration at
the Aiud prison was not given to me. Though my mother went through extensive interrogation meant to link her to propaganda against the regime—specifically, the typing of
the flyers—nothing could be traced to her thanks to both my parents' extra vigilance and
her strenuous denials that she knew about or was implicated in the typing and distribu-
tion. There is detailed information on how my parents purchased the legal and illegal
typewriters and how my father buried the illegal one; there are photos of the typewriter
as it was exhumed by the Securitate while he was under arrest; there are letters and written declarations given by scared people who found anti-Communist propaganda in their
mailboxes and went to the police/Securitate to declare them; photos and maps of where
the anti-Communist flyers were found; a map of my father's demonstration in București;
scientific/criminal fingerprinting of both typewriters; and, among many other things,
written declarations by my father during the interrogation process, which lasted from
March 10 until August 1, 1983, detailing his dissident activities. The tiny sample included
here is restricted to more visual material and his prison sentence.

Page 128

District of Buzău

Securitate office of
the town Rîmnicu-Sărat

Date: 3.2.1981

Exhibit V

PHOTO

Detailed photo
containing a section
of the metal mailboxes
of Bloc 1D Entrance A,
Digului Street, Rîmnicu-
Sărat; shown are the
mailboxes of residents
. . . who found letters
of anti-Communist
propaganda on the dates
of 3.2.1981 at 6:30 and
2.2.81 at 18:15.

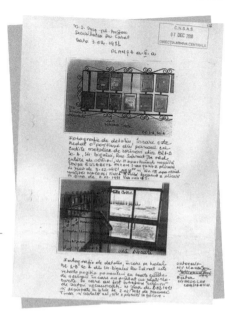

PHOTO

Detailed photo of all the mailboxes in the Bloc 1 D
Entrance A, Digului Street Rîmnicu-Sărat with arrows
indicating the mailboxes of the residents . . . who
found letters on the dates of 2.1.1981 and 2.2.1981.

Material assembled by Major [indecipherable]; photo
credits, Major Nedelcu Constantin

222

The Socialist Republic
of România

The Bucureşti Military
Tribunal

Dossier no. 272, 1983

Minutes of the
sentence no. 324
Today, 1 August 1983

President: Justice
Colonel Mîndrescu
Dumitru

Popular Assessors:
Captain Roşca Gavril,
Captain Taflan Mircea

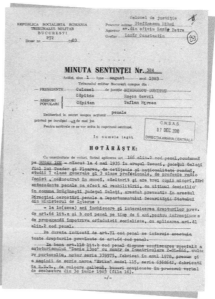

Making deliberations
in secret regarding penal action
against the guilty person named below,

In the name of the law

IT IS DECIDED:

With unanimous votes, applying the article 166
paragraph 2 from the penal code, the tribunal
condemns ION BUGAN, born[12] . . . arrested by the
Department of the Security of State, to:

—ten years in prison and denial of all rights for
six years in conformity with article 64, paragraphs
a and b of the penal code, for *the crime of
propaganda against the socialist regime,* with the
application of article 41, paragraph 2 of the penal
code.

12. Personal information and family situation.

During the period indicated by article 71 of the penal code, all rights provided by article 64 of the penal code are not permitted.

In conformity with article 118, paragraph B of the penal code, we will confiscate the car Dacia 1300 with the license plate number 2GL 666 and the typewriter Erika 115, in addition to all the goods mentioned in the house search document of 30 June 1983 (file 16).

The house will
continue to remain
sealed.

The criminal will
remain under arrest
as from 10 March 1983
and this time will be
deducted from the
full sentence at
the end.

The criminal shall
pay the state the sum
of 2,500 lei for the
lawyer fees and 150
lei for the office
defending lawyer.

He has right to
dispute this sentence
within ten days of this
communication only.

This sentence is
pronounced in the public meeting,
today 1 August 1983.

President . . .   Popular assessors . . .

Signatures, and the CNSAS stamp

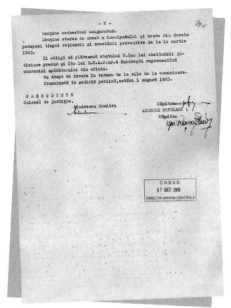

Bread Loaf and the Bakeless Prizes

The Katharine Bakeless Nason Literary Publication Prizes were established in 1995 to expand the Bread Loaf Writers' Conference's commitment to the support of emerging writers. Endowed by the LZ Francis Foundation, the prizes commemorate Middlebury College patron Katharine Bakeless Nason and launch the publication career of a poet, a fiction writer, and a creative nonfiction writer annually. Winning manuscripts are chosen in an open national competition by a distinguished judge in each genre. Winners are published by Graywolf Press.

2011 Judges

Carl Phillips
Poetry

Stacey D'Erasmo
Fiction

Lynn Freed
Creative Nonfiction

CARMEN BUGAN is the author of a collection of poetry, *Crossing the Carpathians*. Her monograph, *Seamus Heaney and East European Poetry in Translation: Poetics of Exile*, is forthcoming. Her work has been published in *Harvard Review*, the *Times Literary Supplement*, and *Modern Poetry in Translation*.

Burying the Typewriter is typeset in Adobe Caslon Pro, a typeface drawn by Carol Twombly in 1989, and based on the work of William Caslon (c. 1692–1766), an English engraver, punchcutter, and typefounder. This book was designed by Ann Sudmeier. Composition by BookMobile Design and Publishing Services, Minneapolis, Minnesota. Manufactured by Versa Press on acid-free 30 percent postconsumer wastepaper.